How To Investigate
Your Friends, Enemies, and Lovers

📖 Books by Trent Sands

Reborn In The U.S.A. (2nd Edition)
Reborn In Canada (2nd Edition)
Reborn Overseas
Reborn with Credit
Personal Privacy Through Foreign Investing
Privacy Power: Protecting Your Personal Privacy
    in the Digital Age

✍ Books by John Q. Newman

The Heavy Duty New Identity
Understanding U.S. Identity Documents
Be Your Own Dick
Credit Power: Restore Your Credit in 90 Days or Less!

📖✍ Books by John Q. Newman **and** Trent Sands

Handbook of Altered and False Identification
Birth Certificate and Social Security Number Fraud

How To Investigate
Your Friends, Enemies, and Lovers

by
Trent Sands
&
John Q. Newman

INDEX
Publishing Group, Inc.
San Diego, California

How To Investigate
Your Friends, Enemies, and Lovers

Published by
INDEX PUBLISHING GROUP, INC.
3368 Governor Drive, Suite 273
San Diego, CA 92122
(619) 455-6100 voice; (619) 552-9050 fax
e-mail: ipgbooks@indexbooks.com
Internet: http://www.indexbooks.com/~ipgbooks

ISBN 1-56866-143-6 (Quality Paperback)
Library of Congress Card Number 95-81312

Cataloging in Publication
(Provided by Quality Books Inc.)

Sands, Trent.
  How to investigate your friends, enemies, & lovers / by Trent
Sands and John Q. Newman.
  p.cm.
  Includes index.
  Preassigned LCCN: 95-81312
  ISBN 1-56866-143-6

  1. Private investigators. 2. Private investigators--Equipment
and supplies--Handbooks, manuals, etc. 3. Newman, John Q. I.
Title.
HV8085.H69 1997

363.2'5
QBI97-40533

Cover design: In house
Text design : In house
Typesetting : Timothy Type
Printed and bound by: SOS Printing, San Diego, CA

Printed in the United States of America
1 2 3 4 5 6 7 8 9

11/98

CONTENTS

3. DRIVER RECORDS 25

4. THE WONDERFUL WORLD OF SOCIAL SECURITY. 36

5. DETERMINING THE SOCIAL SECURITY NUMBER .. 70

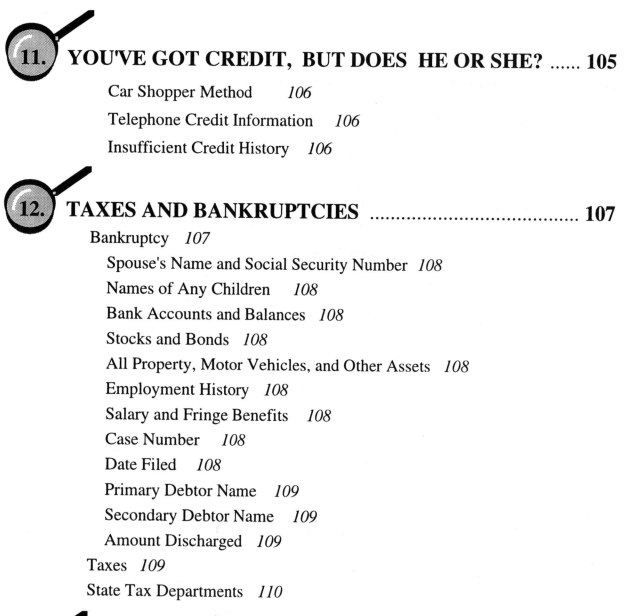

PREFACE

Linda Robertson was a vibrant, 25-year-old intern at a hospital. She had just completed her third year of medical school, and her career was headed upward. She had everything to live for.

Her life as a premed student, and then medical school student, left her little time for socializing or much dating. She accepted the fact that this would have to wait until later.

She rented a small apartment close to the hospital where she worked, sharing her modest digs with another female med school student. Between her eighty hour work weeks and her roommate's schedule, they saw very little of each other.

Across the hallway lived Jim Eiles. Frequently, Jim would pass Linda in the hallway on her way to the hospital or coming home from work. Jim was a good looking man in his early thirties. As time passed the simple greetings in the hallway progressed to small chitchat. Eventually, Jim asked her out on a date, and she accepted.

Jim's story was that he was an attorney working on a case that required him to do research in this city. He seemed to understand the law and his apartment was certainly full of legal books. Their nascent relationship progressed, and eventually she took Jim to meet her family.

Linda's family was pleased that their daughter had finally met a nice man with good career prospects. He was well spoken, polite, and very personable. A few months later, Linda gave up her apartment and moved in with Jim.

The first six months of living together were very good, and Jim proposed to Linda. She accepted his offer without hesitation. They began the process of merging their finances, and then small warning signs gradually began to appear.

Jim never introduced Linda to his family, saying that they were estranged. He never took Linda to his hometown or had her meet his colleagues. A few months later, the small problems blew up into a disaster.

Jim had been made a cosigner on many of Linda's accounts. Linda allowed him to manage the finances because he had the time, and it seemed to her that his legal background would make him a natural to do this.

Jim used his financial authority to apply for numerous credit accounts in Linda's name, accounts she knew nothing about. The credit cards would be sent to another address, and over a short period Jim ran up nearly forty thousand dollars in numerous unpaid bills.

A creditor's telephone call to Linda at work was the only warning she had. Jim assured her it was a mistake and said he would take care of it. After the telephone call, Jim quietly got his things together, and moved out one day when Linda was at work.

A few weeks later, Linda was being besieged with telephone calls from all sorts of creditors too numerous to list. Her credit was ruined, and because Linda had given Jim signing authority over her accounts, she was held liable for the bills.

Had Linda known how to check, she would have found out that "Jim" had pulled this scam many times on women in the last few years. It was how he earned his living. Numerous lawsuits and judgments were outstanding against him in five different states. No criminal prosecution was possible, because Jim always covered his tracks.

Had Linda read this book, and done some simple, easy, and relatively inexpensive checking on Jim, she could have avoided the financial ruin she endured.

This book shows you how to protect yourself against men, or women, or even companies and corporations, who seek to prey on the trusting among us.

This book can also enable you to separate truth from fiction when it comes to public figures and celebrities.

Consider a well-known television actress who has publicly maintained that her parents physically and sexually abused her as a child. This actress also asserts that her father held her infant brother over the side of a gondola on the skyride at a major Southern California amusement park and threatened to drop him.

She made these accusations on national television. She also accused both of her ex-husbands of physically abusing her during her marriages, although before the divorces she had written a book in which her second husband appeared as a great friend and protector.

This book will enable you to investigate the claims celebrities, such as this actress, frequently make to garner sympathy and publicity from the public. In the case of this actress, there is no documentation of any of the claims she has made, and her own family, brothers and sisters included, have publicly refuted her statements on national television.

Another well-known action adventure movie star has gone to great lengths to conceal his past—a past that involved being sympathetic to those who have Nazi views. Although this man is certainly not a Nazi now, he has attempted to remake himself into a wholesome character with an altogether different past.

Remaking oneself is a favorite ploy among Hollywood celebrities. It can involve creating an entirely different past, as in the case of the television actress mentioned, or simply losing a few years by changing the year of birth.

> This book will allow you to find out the real "skinny" on just about *anyone*, using methods that are mostly legal and relatively simple. It could save you from leaving your children with a babysitter who is a convicted child molester or, as Linda could easily have done, finding out if your prospective spouse has a criminal record or a shady past. It's a tough world out there—be safe, not sorry!

Trent Sands

f

John Q. Newman

 # Introduction

The world of the private investigator is a popular topic of television shows and movies. On screen, the investigator is frequently shown in glamorous locales, dodging danger at every turn to ferret out some piece of critical information. That is a Hollywood fantasy.

The real work of private investigators involves little glamour and much less physical danger than that of their celluloid cousins. The key job of an investigator is to locate private information, using a variety of proprietary and public sources. The compilation of this information then allows the "big picture" to be put together, and the case to be solved.

Private investigators work on a myriad of cases, involving everything from locating missing people to finding long forgotten money or other assets, and (of course) discovering whether a spouse is cheating. Investigators can accomplish their work in large part because most records in the United States are remarkably public.

Examples of public records include driver records, voter registration listings, and county property tax data. Private investigators make extensive use of such records, and many others, to accomplish their work. In this book we will show how *you*, without any special licensing or training, can access the same records and perform your own investigations.

What might *you* be interested in investigating? Maybe you don't quite trust your daughter's new boyfriend. Does he have a criminal record or a history of bad driving offenses? With the information in this book, you will learn how to find answers to these questions. Perhaps you are considering a business venture with a new partner who you don't know well. The information in this book will tell you how to determine if he has ever gone bankrupt or is facing lawsuits.

Maybe you're just curious about a celebrity. The methods in this book will allow you to satisfy your desire to learn fascinating private data about your favorite screen or sports star.

How do we begin our study of investigations? The first step is to understand the vast trail of paper records we all create in our daily existence, and learn how these records can be accessed by the public.

The Trails We Leave

The very act of being born creates numerous government and private records. As we grow older, many other records are created about us in computers maintained by government agencies and private corporations. When these records are taken in sum, they form a "trail" that reveals much about our lives. Where we lived, what type of education we obtained, who we married, what we owned, and on and on. The record keeping continues on past death. The state says we are not officially gone until a death certificate is issued in our name, and the Social Security Administration keeps a file on us long after we have departed this planet.

The following list is just a partial sample of the records the average individual will have generated by the time they are about 25 years old.

- ◆ BIRTH REGISTRATION

- ◆ DRIVING RECORD

- ◆ VOTER REGISTRATION RECORDS

- ◆ SOCIAL SECURITY RECORDS

- ◆ PROPERTY TAX RECORDS

- ◆ CREDIT BUREAU RECORDS

- ◆ WORKERS' COMPENSATION RECORDS

These types of records have existed for many years, but recent advances in technology have allowed them to be computerized and made accessible. Searching out voter records used to be a long and time consuming process. The same was true of courthouse records. The computer changed all of this. These records, and many others, can often be accessed via computer without even leaving your home.

When records from different sources are combined, a comprehensive dossier can be created on an individual. What kind of car does the person drive? Does his driving record show a lot of speeding tickets or a drunk driving conviction? How much is his house worth, and who holds the mortgage? What is his Social Security Number and where has he lived over the last ten years? Does he have good credit, or is he a deadbeat? Does he *really* have a college degree? These are just a few examples of what you can unearth.

The key to developing a complete background file on an individual is to search each source of information completely, making sure you have exhausted that source before moving on. Little items, seemingly of small importance, can later prove to be the key to opening the door to larger sources of personal data.

For the novice, the best method is to work from the present, and go backwards. Many records are compiled on a local basis, be it city or county. The beauty of local records is that they are almost always open to the public, and being local records, they are nearby.

As we go through this book, we will assume that you are investigating a particular subject—a thirty-five-year-old male with whom you are considering entering into a business partnership or personal relationship (it could as easily have been a female, of course). The only information you have at present is his name and approximate age. With only this information you will be able to assemble a total file on him by following the steps outlined in the following chapters.

2

Local Information Sources

The actor had labored for years in obscurity. Small parts, unremarkable dialogue, and sleeping on friend's couches. Finally, his breakthrough role came, and now the media was everywhere. He had seen how privacy was the first casualty of the movie business, and he was determined not to surrender his. He did not want to become a tabloid fixture, a caricature of a real person.

He thought he had taken all of the necessary steps so he could still come and go from his modest home quietly. He was not part of the Hollywood party circuit, and did not live an ostentatious lifestyle. He was determined that his relationship with his girlfriend would not be torn apart by the media.

His illusion was shattered early one morning. He opened his front door, still dressed for bed, and the paparazzi were there, snapping his picture with abandon. How had they found out where he lived? Even his neighbors did not know who he was.

With only a name and address, anyone can assemble a great deal of information from local records. The first step is to identify the name, and then locate an address for that name. To do this you will first consult one of the most useful, yet often overlooked, sources of information—the telephone directory. Telephone directory information can be accessed two ways. The first is the tried and true way of consulting the phone book for the city and metropolitan area where you live for a listing in the subject's name.

When working this way, if you do not have a good idea what part of town your subject resides in, you need to be careful that you have covered the entire metropolitan area. This search should net you a short list, depending on how common his name is, of numbers and addresses that *could be* his.

The other method of searching telephone listings involves using one of the computerized telephone information products now available. Two of the most common are **Phonedisc** and **Phonefile** (see *Resource List* at the end of this book). These listings cover the entire nation and are available on CD-ROM. Many public libraries subscribe to these telephone products. The beauty of searching on these systems is that you can search a broad area very quickly. These systems allow you to search by name or by address. A search can be limited by zip code, area code, city, or state.

If your subject has a listed number, we should now have a specific address to work from. Even if we did not turn up an address or telephone number via the phone search, we can still obtain this through the local county records. Before we go into the records we will search, we need to examine what records are available at the county level and where they're held.

Property records are the largest single source of county records. All property in a given county is subject to assessment for tax purposes, so county recorders maintain very detailed files on all property and property owners. Every time a piece of property is bought or sold, or improvements are made, or a new appraisal is made, a file will be created at the county recorder's office.

Voter registration records are also maintained at the county level. A county elections board, or an organization with a similar name, will maintain the voting list for the county. The beauty of voter registration records is that they are filed by name and are county-wide in scope. If your subject is registered to vote in the county, you will obtain his address. A voter registration record will contain the following data in most jurisdictions:

- ◆ FULL NAME OF VOTER

- ◆ CURRENT RESIDENTIAL ADDRESS

- ◆ BIRTHDATE

- ◆ TELEPHONE NUMBER

- ◆ SOCIAL SECURITY OR STATE ID CARD NUMBER

Voter registration records are available by mail. Call or write to the local county board of elections to find out the current fee, if any, for a record search. Send your request in the form of a letter to the elections board with the fee attached. Within two weeks you should receive a response.

Returning to the county property tax records, if your subject owns any property in the county under his name, a search of the county tax records will reveal it. A typical property tax record will contain some derivative of the following information:

- ◆ FULL NAME OF PROPERTY OWNER

- ◆ LOCATION OF PROPERTY

- DESCRIPTION OF PROPERTY

- VALUE OF THE PROPERTY

- YEAR PURCHASED

- MORTGAGE HOLDER

- TELEPHONE NUMBER OF OWNER

- ADDRESS FOR TAX BILLS

County property tax information can be accessed via letter to the tax assessor's office, or by an alternative method. **TRW** is a private company that maintains a comprehensive listing of property ownership and tax records. This is called **TRW REDI** Property Data and is used by banks and mortgage lenders. Many public libraries will have TRW REDI property data available on microfiche for their county. The listing will contain the same information given in county tax records. The advantage of using the TRW information is that it is quicker to obtain and easier to read.

County records also include licensing information for a variety of occupations and businesses. If your subject owns a business, you can obtain a copy of the business license. If the business is not incorporated, a **Fictitious Business Name Statement** will be on file with the county. This document will contain the names, addresses, and sometimes birthdates and Social Security numbers of the true owners of the business.

Don't forget things like pet licenses. It may seem trivial, but these applications contain a lot of information.

The next source of county information we will consider are noncriminal records at the county courthouse. Any legal action that has been filed will be available here, and as such, it is now a public record. The following is a partial listing of some of the legal records you may find at the county courthouse:

- NOTICE OF STATE TAX LIEN

- DIVORCE DECREE

- CHANGE OF NAME

- GARNISHMENT ORDER

- POWER OF ATTORNEY

- CIVIL JUDGMENT

- LIEN

- INCOMPETENCY HEARING

- SATISFACTION OF MORTGAGE

- QUIT CLAIM DEED

- CHILD SUPPORT AGREEMENT

A search of records under your subject's name at the county courthouse may reveal that he has lawsuits pending against him, has child support obligations, or has unpaid state taxes. These records can be obtained from the Clerk of the Court. In many counties there is no fee for a name search of the civil judgment files. Contact the Clerk of the Court directly in your city for the rules in your area.

Local court records are also accessible via third party **information brokers**. These brokers compile abstracts from the local court records and put them on computer (some of the best are in the *Resource List*). The information broker, for a price, can provide you with the information faster. We will discuss when to use information brokers in greater detail later in the book.

What results should our investigation of "Mr. X" have yielded so far? We should now know his full name, current address, and perhaps his birthdate or Social Security Number. Even if we do not have all of this data now, we are well on our way to knowing almost everything about him.

Driver Records

A member of a prominent political family was accused of a vicious sexual assault. The entire case rested on the testimony of the victim. There were no witnesses to the alleged assault and no physical evidence to link the suspect to the crime.

It was a case that would depend entirely on the credibility of the victim and the suspect. The suspect's attorneys needed to find a way to destroy the victim's credibility. A search of her driving record provided just the data they were looking for.

Over the last few years she had been in traffic court more than twenty times on various charges from reckless driving to DUI. Her license had been suspended, and thousands of dollars in traffic fines were outstanding. This was just the ammunition the defense attorneys needed.

The next step on our investigation odyssey will involve accessing our subject's driver's license and vehicle registration records. Most Americans have a driver's license, hence the utility of driver records. In nearly all states, driver record information is open to the public. The information available from state motor vehicle departments consists of three main types:

- ◆ LICENSE OR ID APPLICATION FILE

- ◆ DRIVING RECORD

- ◆ VEHICLE REGISTRATION INFORMATION

The license application file will contain the information provided when seeking a license or state identity card. Test scores, type of identification documents provided, and previous license history will be located here.

The driving record will be a chronological history of the subject's driving performance from the time he initially obtained a license in the state. All moving violations, traffic court citations, and impaired driving charges will be reflected on this document. This information is used by insurance companies to determine rates on new and renewal automobile insurance policies.

The vehicle registration file will contain details of the vehicles owned by the subject. Data such as registration number and lienholder information can be found on these documents.

The following information can be determined from driving record information:

- FULL NAME

- BIRTHDATE

- SOCIAL SECURITY NUMBER (IN SOME STATES)

- HEIGHT AND WEIGHT

- SEX

- EYE AND HAIR COLOR

- ADDRESS

- MOVING VIOLATION RECORDS

- ACCIDENT RECORDS

Some states will provide you with a copy of the license itself, along with copies of all application forms completed. The primary benefit of motor vehicle department records is that they allow you to ascertain **primary identifiers** on the individual, such as the birthdate and Social Security Number.

The way you access these records is to write to the state motor vehicle department in the state capitol. In your letter ask for a *Driving Record Request Form*. Most states have a standard form that they prefer you to use when requesting driver license information. This form will also tell you what the current fee is for a search. Use of the form will ensure that your request is processed faster.

There are three ways a license history request can be made. They are the following:

- BY LICENSE NUMBER

- BY SOCIAL SECURITY NUMBER

- BY NAME ONLY

The easiest search is done with the license number. It is unlikely you will have your subject's license number, so you will be forced to do a search by just his name or his name and birthdate. A search by name only is called an **alphabetical search**. The problem with this kind of search is that, if his name is a common one, there may be hundreds of files that potentially could be his.

Attempt to narrow the search down as much as possible by using the information you located in the county records to pinpoint the most probable candidate.

Another useful information source from the motor vehicle department is the **vehicle registration record file**. The amount of detail varies from state to state, but in some states the vehicle registration certificate will contain more information than the license itself. In Ohio, for example, the vehicle registration certificate will contain the following information:

♦ FULL NAME OF REGISTERED OWNER

♦ ADDRESS OF REGISTERED OWNER

♦ NAME OF LIENHOLDER

♦ ADDRESS OF LIENHOLDER

♦ VEHICLE REGISTRATION NUMBER

♦ VEHICLE SERIAL NUMBER

♦ VEHICLE TITLE NUMBER

♦ SOCIAL SECURITY NUMBER OF OWNER

♦ BIRTHDATE OF OWNER

The last types of motor-vehicle-related records you may wish to obtain are **accident reports**. If your subject's driving record indicates that he has been involved in an accident, you should obtain the full accident report. Accident reports will often contain additional telephone numbers, addresses, and personal data you may not already have.

Accident reports are not maintained by the motor vehicle department. They are maintained by the local police in the jurisdiction where the accident occurred and usually by the state police. A complete list of all state police departments starts on the next page.

STATE POLICE DEPARTMENTS

Accident reports will generally be on file with the state police even if the accident was handled by a local police department. Write to the following agencies asking for a *Records Request Form*, what information is required to obtain an accident report, and what if any fees are required.

STATE POLICE

ALABAMA

Alabama Department of
Public Safety
Post Office Box 1511
Montgomery, AL 36192

ALASKA

Department of Public Safety
Post Office Box N
Juneau, AK 99811

ARIZONA

Department of Public Safety
2102 West Encanto Boulevard
Phoenix, AZ 85005

ARKANSAS

Department of Public Safety
Three Natural Resources Drive
Little Rock, AR 72215

CALIFORNIA

State Department of Justice
Post Office Box 94425
Sacramento, CA 94244

COLORADO

Colorado Bureau of Investigations
690 Kipling Street
Lakewood, CO 80215

CONNECTICUT

State Police Department
294 Colony Street
Meriden, CT 06450

DELAWARE

State Police Department
Post Office Box 430
Dover, DE 19903

DISTRICT OF COLUMBIA

Department of Public Safety
Post Office Box 1606
Washington, D.C. 20013

FLORIDA

Department of Law Enforcement
Post Office Box 1489
Tallahassee, FL 32302

GEORGIA

Department of State Police
Post Office Box 370748
Decatur, GA 30037

HAWAII

Department of Public Safety
465 South King Street
Honolulu, HI 96813

IDAHO

Department of State Police
6083 Clinton Street
Boise, ID 83704

ILLINOIS

Department of State Police
260 North Chicago Street
Joliet, IL 60431

INDIANA

Indiana State Police
100 North Senate Avenue
Indianapolis, IN 46204

IOWA

Department of Public Safety
Wallace State Office Building
Des Moines, IA 50319

KANSAS

Kansas Bureau of Public Safety
1620 Southwest Tyler
Topeka, KS 66612

KENTUCKY

Kentucky State Police
1250 Louisville Road
Frankfort, KY 40601

LOUISIANA

Department of Public Safety
Post Office Box 66614
Baton Rouge, LA 70896

MAINE

Maine State Police
36 Hospital Street
Augusta, ME 04330

MARYLAND

Maryland State Police
1201 Reisterstown Road
Pikesville, MD 21208

MASSACHUSETTS

Department of Public Safety
One Ashburton Place
Boston, MA 02108

MICHIGAN

Department of State Police
714 South Harrison Road
East Lansing, MI, 48823

MINNESOTA

Department of Public Safety
1246 University Avenue
Saint Paul, MN 55104

MISSISSIPPI

Department of Public Safety
Post Office Box 958
Jackson, MI 39205

MISSOURI

Department of Public Safety
1510 East Elm Street
Jefferson City, MS 65102

MONTANA

Department of State Police
303 North Roberts
Helena, MO 59620

NEBRASKA

Nebraska State Police
Post Office Box 94907
Lincoln, NE 68509

NEVADA

Department of Public Safety
555 Wright Way
Carson City, NV 89711

NEW HAMPSHIRE

New Hampshire State Police
10 Hazen Drive
Concord, NH 03305

NEW JERSEY

New Jersey State Police
Post Office Box 7068
West Trenton, NJ 08628

NEW MEXICO

Department of Public Safety
Post Office Box 1628
Santa Fe, NM 87504

NEW YORK

New York State Police
Executive Park Tower
Albany, NY 12203

NORTH CAROLINA

Department of Public Safety
407 Blount Street
Raleigh, NC 27602

NORTH DAKOTA

North Dakota Bureau of
Investigation
Post Office Box 1054
Bismarck, ND 58502

OHIO

Department of Investigations
Post Office Box 365
London, OH 43140

OKLAHOMA

Department of Public Safety
Post Office Box 11497
Oklahoma City, OK 73176

OREGON

Oregon State Police
3772 Portland Road
Salem, OR 97310

PENNSYLVANIA

Pennsylvania State Police
1800 Elmerton Avenue
Harrisburg, PA 17110

RHODE ISLAND

Department of Public Safety
72 Pine Street
Providence, RI 02903

SOUTH CAROLINA

Department of Law Enforcement
Post Office Box 21398
Columbia, SC 29221

SOUTH DAKOTA

Division of Criminal Investigation
500 East Capitol Avenue
Pierre, SD 57501

31

TENNESSEE

Department of Public Safety
1150 Foster Avenue
Nashville, TN 37224

TEXAS

Texas State Police
Post Office Box 4143
Austin, TX 78765

UTAH

Department of Public Safety
4501 South 2700 West Avenue
Salt Lake City, UT 84119

VERMONT

Vermont State Police
103 South Main Street
Waterbury, VT 05676

VIRGINIA

State Police of Virginia
Post Office Box 27272
Richmond, VA 23261

WASHINGTON

Washington State Police
Post Office Box 2527
Olympia, WA 98504

WEST VIRGINIA

West Virginia State Police
752 Jefferson Road
South Charleston, WV 25309

WISCONSIN

Wisconsin Law Enforcement
Bureau
Post Office Box 2718
Madison, WI 53701

WYOMING

Criminal Investigations Bureau
316 West 22nd Street
Cheyenne, WY 85002

MOTOR VEHICLE DEPARTMENT ADDRESSES

The addresses of all state motor vehicle departments follow. Always call first to obtain current fee information.

ALABAMA

Department of Public Safety
Driver License Division
PO Box 1471
Montgomery, AL 36192
334-272-8868

ALASKA

Department of Public Safety
Pouch N
Juneau, AK 99811
907-465-4364

ARIZONA
Motor Vehicle Division
1801 West Jefferson
Phoenix, AZ 85009
602-255-0072

ARKANSAS
Office of Driver Services
PO Box 1272
Little Rock, AR 72203
501-371-1743

CALIFORNIA
Department of Motor Vehicles
Driver License Division
PO Box 12590
Sacramento, CA 95813
916-445-6236

COLORADO
Motor Vehicle Division
140 West Sixth Avenue
Denver, CO 80204
303-866-3407

CONNECTICUT
Department of Motor Vehicles
60 State Street
Wetherfield, CT 06109
203-566-3300

DELAWARE
Motor Vehicle Division
PO Box 698
Highway Administration Building
Dover, DE 19901
302-736-4497

DISTRICT OF COLUMBIA
Department of Motor Vehicles
301 C Street NW
Washington, DC 20001
202-727-6679

FLORIDA
Division of Drivers Licenses
Department of Highway Safety
Neil Kirkman Building
Tallahassee, FL 32201
904-488-3411

GEORGIA
Department of Public Safety
PO Box 1456
Atlanta, GA 30371
404-656-5890

HAWAII
Motor Vehicle Office
Department of Transportation
869 Punchbowl Street
Honolulu, HI 96813
808-548-3205

IDAHO
Motor Vehicle Bureau
PO Box 34
Boise, ID 83731
208-334-2586

ILLINOIS
Department of Motor Vehicles
2701 Dirksen Parkway
Springfield, IL 62723
217-782-6212

INDIANA

Bureau of Motor Vehicles
Room 4021
State Office Building
Indianapolis, IN 45204
317-232-2798

IOWA

Department of Transportation
Office of Driver License
Lucas State Office Building
Des Moines, IA 50319
515-281-5649

KANSAS

Department of Revenue
Division of Vehicles
State Office Building
Topeka, KS 66626
913-296-3601

KENTUCKY

Division of Driver Licensing
State Office Building
Frankfort, KY 40622
502-564-6800

LOUISIANA

Department of Public Safety
Office of Motor Vehicles
PO Box 64886
Baton Rouge, LA 70896
504-925-6343

MAINE

Division of Motor Vehicles
Augusta, ME 04333
207-289-3583

MARYLAND

Motor Vehicle Administration
6601 Ritchie Highway
Glen Burnie, MD 21062
301-768-1855

MASSACHUSETTS

Registry of Motor Vehicles
100 Nashua Street
Boston, MA 02114
617-727-3700

MICHIGAN

Bureau of Driver Records
Secondary Complex
Lansing, MI 48918
517-322-1460

MINNESOTA

Driver Licensing Division
161 Transportation Building
St. Paul, MN 55155
612-296-6000

MISSISSIPPI

Department of Public Safety
PO Box 958
Jackson, MS 39205
601-982-1212

MISSOURI

Driver License Bureau
PO Box 200
Jefferson City, MO 65101
314-751-2733

MONTANA
Drivers Services
303 North Roberts
Helena, MT 59620
402-471-2281

NEVADA
Driver License Division
555 Wright Way
Carson City, NV 89711
702-885-5360

NEW HAMPSHIRE
Divsion of Motor Vehicles
Hazen Drive
Concord, NH 03301
603-271-2371

NEW JERSEY
Division of Motor Vehicles
25 South Montgomery Street
Trenton, NJ 08666
609-292-9849

NEW MEXICO
Motor Vehicle Division
Manuel Lujan Building
Santa Fe, NM 87503
505-827-2362

NEW YORK
License Production Bureau
PO Box 2688
Empire State Plaza
Albany, NY 12220
518-474-2068

NORTH CAROLINA
Division of Motor Vehicles
1100 New Bern Avenue
Raleigh, NC 27697
916-733-4241

NORTH DAKOTA
State Licensing Division
Capitol Grounds
Bismark, ND 58505
701-224-4353

OHIO
Bureau of Motor Vehicles
4300 Kimberly Parkway
Columbus, OH 43227
614-466-7666

OKLAHOMA
Department of Public Safety
3600 North Eastern
Oklahoma City, OK 73136
405-424-0411

OREGON
Motor Vehicle Department
1905 Lana Avenue NE
Salem, OR 97301
503-378-6994

PENNSYLVANIA
Bureau of Driver Licensing
Commonwealth and Forestry
Harrisburg, PA 17122
717-787-3130

RHODE ISLAND
Division of Motor Vehicles
State Office Building
Providence, RI 02903
401-277-3000

SOUTH CAROLINA
Motor Vehicle Division
Drawer 1498
Columbia, SC 29216
803-758-3201

SOUTH DAKOTA
Department of Public Safety
118 West Capitol
Pierre, SD 57501
605-773-3191

TENNESSEE
Driver License
Andrew Jackson Building
Nashville, TN 37210
615-741-3954

TEXAS
Department of Public Safety
PO Box 4087
Austin, TX 78773
512-465-2000

UTAH
Driver License Division
4501 South 2700 West
Salt Lake City, UT 84119
801-965-4400

VERMONT
Department of Motor Vehicles
Montpelier, VT 05602
802- 828-2121

VIRGINIA
Department of Motor Vehicles
PO Box 27412
Richmond, VA 23269
804- 257-0406

WASHINGTON
Department of Licensing
Highway Building
Olympia, WA 98504
206-753-6977

WEST VIRGINIA
Department of Motor Vehicles
1800 Washington Street East
Charleston, WV 25317
304-348-2719

WISCONSIN
Division of Motor Vehicles
4802 Sheboygan Avenue
Madison, WI 53702
608-266-2325

WYOMING
Motor Vehicle Division
2200 Carey Avenue
Cheyenne, WY 82002
307-777-7971

4

The Wonderful World of Social Security

They had been best friends from the day they met in Air Force basic training in 1955. For the first six years of their service, they had kept in contact regularly. Later, as new wives and other commitments grew, they lost contact with each other. The one friend served his twenty years and retired in 1975, the other stayed on active duty for another ten years.

After the second friend retired, he began to wonder what had happened with his old buddy. All he had was his name and Social Security Number. His wife knew someone who located missing people with computers. She asked for his help. A day later he had his old buddy's current address and telephone number.

In any investigation, learning the subject's Social Security Number (SSN) is an invaluable tool. From the SSN we can determine if the individual has the background he says he has, where he has lived over the last ten years, if he is the age he claims, and we can also access many other databases and record systems that contain additional information.

We first need to understand exactly what an SSN is, how it is assigned, and what each part of the number means.

The Social Security System was created to ensure that every working American would have a minimal retirement income. When Social Security was introduced in the 1930s, many people had no retirement or pension plan with their employers. The Great Depression was fresh in people's minds, and the idea of a national pension system made good sense.

The Federal government would be responsible for administering the system and collecting the payroll taxes from both employers and employees. Each worker would be assigned an account number, to which the accumulated contributions would be posted. This money, along with the accumulated interest, would be held in trust by the government until the worker retired. Upon retirement, the worker would receive a predetermined level of monthly benefits. The reality today is diametrically opposed to the initial scheme. All current contributions into Social Security are paid out immediately to existing retirees, and the trust fund faces a perennial deficit.

The Social Security law required that the Federal government devise an identification system that could keep track of nearly every person in the nation. A unique numerical identification had to be designed that would allow many people with the same names and birthdates to be clearly separated in government records. The Social Security law required, for the first time, that the Federal government in the United States keep a file on practically every citizen.

The uniqueness of the SSN as an identifier led to its use as an indexing tool in the files of many other government and private organizations.

The law mandates that the following organizations use Social Security Numbers as a file identification tool:

◆ THE U.S. ARMED FORCES: SSN IS SERVICE SERIAL NUMBER

◆ INTERNAL REVENUE SERVICE: SSN IDENTIFIES RETURN

◆ PASSPORT OFFICE: SSN MUST BE PROVIDED

◆ FEDERAL EMPLOYEES PERSONNEL RECORDS USE SSN

◆ WELFARE AND ENTITLEMENT PROGRAMS TRACK BY SSN

The Social Security Number must be used as an identifier for the above programs. It can be, and often is, an identifier by individual states for documents such as driver's licenses and voter registration cards.

Private organizations also make extensive use of the number. Insurance companies frequently request the SSN to allow rapid access to customer files, and credit bureaus use the SSN as a file identification tool. Banks and brokerage firms are required to obtain the number to use on interest reporting forms that must be sent to the Internal Revenue Service each year on all customers.

How can the SSN be used to identify so many millions of people uniquely? The secret lies in how the number for each individual is created. The nine-digit Social Security Number is composed of three discrete parts, and each reveals something important about the holder.

AREA NUMBERS

The first three digits of the Social Security Number are called **area numbers**. The area number indicates in which state an individual applied for his or her Social Security card. The following area numbers are in active use:

001 to 595

600 to 649

700 to 728

Each state is assigned a certain range of area numbers based on its population. A small state will be assigned fewer area numbers than a large state. The state of Texas is assigned area numbers between 449 to 467 and 627 to 645. By contrast, the state of Wyoming is assigned only one area number, 520.

So the first step in checking out the background of someone is determining if the state of issue of their SSN fits with the geographical history they have given you. There may be a plausible explanation for someone with an Oregon area number having never really lived in the state of Oregon, but further checking should be done. Frequently, people who are attempting to jettison a problem-filled past make minor alterations in the spelling of their names, but continue using the same Social Security Number.

The first chart at the end of this chapter lists the states associated with each active area number. A mention should be made of the 700 to 728 area numbers. These numbers were issued to people receiving railroad retirement benefits from the Federal government. The last time a 700-band area number was issued was in 1980. A few hundred thousand 700-band area numbers were issued between 1976 and 1980 to refugees from the Vietnam War. Other than this small group of Asians, everyone possessing 700 to 728 area numbers will be of retirement age.

GROUP NUMBERS

The middle two numbers of the SSN are known as **group numbers**. The group number can help you to determine if a SSN was ever actually issued. It can also allow you to determine approximately what year the individual received his Social Security Number. We need to understand how the group numbers are assigned.

Group numbers range from 01 to 99. These numbers are not assigned in a straight numerical order. The Social Security Administration uses an *odd-even-even-odd* system to assign these numbers. Here is how it works.

The first group numbers to be assigned for a given area are the odd groups under ten. So, for the 700 area, by example, the first groups to be assigned would be 01, 03, 05, 07, and 09. Once 09 is reached, the even groups between 10 and 99 are assigned. After that the even groups less than 10 are issued, and finally the odd groups above 10 are assigned.

Very often, fake Social Security cards will have valid area numbers but will use group numbers that are not yet activated.

SERIAL NUMBERS

The last four digits of the Social Security Number are collectively called the **serial number**. Serial numbers will range from 0001 to 9999.

For each group within a given area, there are 9,999 possible Social Security Numbers. The first number issued in that group will end with 0001, and the last number with 9999. Let's look at some Social Security Numbers and see how this works.

The first SSN issued in the 700 area would be:

> 700-01-0001

When this group is used up the last number issued within the 01 group would be:

> 700-01-9999

The number that would follow this, according to the odd-even-even-odd rule would be:

> 700-03-0001

The last possible SSN that could theoretically be issued within the 700 area range would be:

> 700-99-9999.

When the areas assigned to a state have been used up, the Social Security Administration must then assign or create new area numbers. This has happened in the last decade. A few states, such as Texas and California, had nearly exhausted their supply of area numbers. So the 600 area band was activated to fill these states' needs.

The second chart at the end of this chapter lists the highest assigned group numbers for all active areas. If we are able to determine that the Social Security Number we have is potentially valid and it has an active group number, we may want to check the number out further. Is that twenty-two-year-old man using a number that was issued in the 1950's? *If he is, the number can not belong to him.* How can we check this?

A few years ago the Social Security Administration published a table of Social Security Numbers that had been issued between 1951 and 1978. These charts are reproduced at the end of this chapter. The way to determine the year of issue of a particular number is to consult the area number at the left side of the chart. Then follow the column over until you find the group number you have been given. The number at the top will be the year it was issued.

If you have determined that a particular SSN is probably valid, you will want to start centering part of your background search in that region. Check the records we have mentioned already, as well as records we will look at later, even if the individual has given you no information that would link him to the area.

If you have not been able to find the Social Security Number of the individual from the record sources you have already consulted, the next chapter will be of critical importance. The methods it describes will allow you to quickly obtain the Social Security Number of almost any adult in the United States.

SOCIAL SECURITY AREA NUMBERS CHART

LOCATION	_AREA NUMBER_
ALABAMA	416-424
ALASKA	574
ARIZONA	526-527
ARKANSAS	429-432
CALIFORNIA	545-573 and 602-626
COLORADO	521-524
CONNECTICUT	040-049
DELAWARE	221-222
DISTRICT OF COLUMBIA	577-579
FLORIDA	261-267 and 589-595
GEORGIA	252-260
HAWAII	575-576
IDAHO	518-519
ILLINOIS	318-361
INDIANA	303-317
IOWA	478-485
KANSAS	509-515
KENTUCKY	400-407
LOUISIANA	433-439
MAINE	004-007
MARYLAND	212-220
MASSACHUSETTS	010-034
MICHIGAN	362-386
MINNESOTA	468-477
MISSISSIPPI	425-428 and 587-588
MISSOURI	486-500
MONTANA	516-517

LOCATION	AREA NUMBER
NEBRASKA	505-508
NEVADA	530
NEW HAMPSHIRE	001-003
NEW JERSEY	135-158
NEW MEXICO	525, 585, and 648-649
NEW YORK	050-134
NORTH CAROLINA	232 and 237-246
NORTH DAKOTA	501-502
OHIO	268-302
OKLAHOMA	440-448
OREGON	540-544
PENNSYLVANIA	159-211
RHODE ISLAND	035-039
SOUTH CAROLINA	247-251
SOUTH DAKOTA	503-504
TENNESSEE	408-415
TEXAS	449-467 and 627-645
UTAH	528-529
VERMONT	008-009
VIRGINIA	223-231
WASHINGTON	531-539
WEST VIRGINIA	223-231
WISCONSIN	387-399
WYOMING	520
VIRGIN ISLANDS	580
PUERTO RICO	580-584
GUAM/AMERICAN SAMOA	586
RAILROAD RETIREMENT	700-728
MARIANNAS ISLANDS/ PHILLIPINES	586

SOCIAL SECURITY GROUP NUMBER CHART

The following chart lists the highest group numbers in use for all active Social Security Numbers. When using the chart remember the odd-even-even-odd system used in assigning group numbers. See the section on Social Security numbers for a full explanation. The first column lists the area number and the second column lists the highest corresponding group number in use.

AREA NUMBER	GROUP NUMBER
001-002	84
003	82
004-007	92
008-009	76
010-015	76
016-034	74
035	62
036-039	60
040-043	90
044-049	88
050-084	80
085-134	78
135-151	92
152-158	90
159-162	74
163-211	72
212-219	35
220	33
221	82
222	80
223-225	65
226-231	63
232	39
233-236	39
237-241	73
242-246	71
247-249	89

AREA NUMBER	GROUP NUMBER
250-251	87
252-255	83
256-260	81
261-267	99
268-302	94
303	13
304-317	11
318-359	86
360-361	84
362	15
363-386	13
387-399	08
400-406	43
407	41
408-412	71
413-415	69
416-420	39
421-424	37
425-428	73
429-432	81
433-439	83
440-448	02
449-467	99
468-477	25
478-485	21
486-500	06
501-502	19
503-504	21
505	31
506-508	29
509-515	06
516-517	25

AREA NUMBER	GROUP NUMBER
518-519	41
520	31
521-524	85
525	97
526-527	99
528-529	99
530	67
531-539	27
540-544	41
545-573	99
574	13
575-576	63
577-579	25
580	31
581-584	99
585	95
586	13
587	73
588	03
589-595	25
596-599	38
600-601	21
602-626	62
627-645	34
646-647	14
648-649	01
700-723	18
724	28
725-726	18
727	10
728	14

Geographical and Chronological Social Security Numbers

YEAR

STATE OR POSSESSION	AREA	51	52	53	54	55	56	57	58	59	60	61	62	63	64	65	66	67	68	69	70	71	72	73	74	75	76	77	78
NEW HAMPSHIRE	001	26	26	28	28	28	30	32	32	32	32	34	36	36	38	40	42	42	44	46	46	48	48	54	56	56	58	60	60
	002	26	26	26	28	28	30	30	30	32	32	34	34	34	38	38	40	40	42	44	44	46	46	48	52	54	56	60	60
	003	24	26	26	26	28	28	30	30	32	32	32	34	38	38	38	40	42	42	44	46	46	48	52	54	56	58	58	58
MAINE	004	32	34	36	36	38	40	40	40	42	42	44	46	50	50	50	52	54	56	56	58	60	62	66	68	70	72	72	74
	005	32	34	34	36	38	40	40	40	42	42	44	44	48	48	50	52	54	54	56	58	60	62	64	66	68	70	72	72
	006	32	34	34	34	36	38	40	40	40	42	44	44	48	48	50	52	54	54	56	58	60	62	64	66	68	70	72	72
	007	32	32	34	34	36	38	38	40	40	42	42	44	46	48	50	50	52	54	56	58	58	60	64	66	68	70	70	72
VERMONT	008	24	24	26	28	28	28	30	30	30	32	32	34	36	36	38	40	40	42	42	44	46	46	54	54	58	60	60	60
	009	22	24	24	24	26	28	28	28	30	30	32	32	34	36	38	38	40	40	42	44	46	46	52	54	56	58	58	58
MASSACHUSETTS	010	28	28	28	30	30	30	32	32	32	34	34	36	38	38	40	42	42	44	46	46	48	48	50	52	54	54	58	58
	011	26	28	28	30	30	30	32	32	32	34	34	36	38	38	40	42	42	44	46	46	48	48	50	52	54	54	58	58
	012	26	28	28	28	28	30	32	32	32	34	34	36	38	38	40	42	42	44	46	46	48	48	50	52	54	54	58	58
	013	28	28	28	28	30	30	32	32	32	34	34	36	38	38	40	42	42	44	46	46	48	48	50	52	54	54	56	58
	014	26	28	28	28	30	30	32	32	32	34	34	36	38	38	40	42	42	44	46	46	48	48	50	52	54	54	56	58
	015	26	28	28	28	30	30	30	32	32	34	34	34	38	38	40	42	42	44	44	46	48	48	50	52	54	54	56	58
	016	28	28	28	28	30	30	30	32	32	32	34	34	38	38	40	42	42	44	46	46	48	48	50	52	54	54	56	58
	017	26	28	28	28	30	30	30	32	32	32	34	36	38	38	40	42	42	44	46	46	48	48	50	52	54	54	56	58
	018	26	28	28	28	30	30	30	32	32	32	34	34	36	38	40	42	42	44	44	46	48	48	50	52	54	54	56	58
	019	26	28	28	28	30	30	30	32	32	32	34	34	36	38	40	40	42	44	44	46	48	48	50	52	54	54	56	58
	020	26	28	28	28	30	30	30	32	32	32	34	34	38	38	40	40	42	44	44	46	48	48	50	52	54	54	56	58
	021	26	28	28	28	30	30	30	32	32	32	34	34	36	38	40	40	42	44	44	46	48	48	50	52	52	54	54	58
	022	26	26	28	28	30	30	30	32	32	32	34	34	36	38	40	40	42	44	44	46	48	48	50	52	52	54	56	58
	023	26	28	28	28	28	30	30	30	32	32	34	34	36	38	38	40	42	42	44	46	48	48	50	52	52	54	56	58
	024	26	26	28	28	28	30	30	30	32	32	34	34	36	38	38	40	42	42	44	46	48	48	50	52	52	54	56	58
	025	26	26	28	28	28	30	30	30	32	32	34	34	36	38	38	40	42	42	44	46	48	48	50	52	52	54	56	58

CONTINUED...

Geographical and Chronological Social Security Numbers

YEAR

STATE OR POSSESSION	AREA	51	52	53	54	55	56	57	58	59	60	61	62	63	64	65	66	67	68	69	70	71	72	73	74	75	76	77	78
MASSACHUSETTS (CONTINUED)	026	26	26	28	28	28	30	30	30	32	32	34	34	36	38	38	40	42	42	44	46	46	48	50	52	52	54	56	58
	027	26	26	28	28	28	30	30	30	32	32	32	34	36	38	38	40	42	42	44	46	46	48	50	52	52	54	56	58
	028	26	26	28	28	28	30	30	30	32	32	32	34	36	38	38	40	40	42	44	46	46	48	50	52	52	54	56	58
	029	26	26	28	28	28	30	30	30	32	32	32	34	36	38	38	40	42	42	44	46	48	48	50	52	52	54	56	56
	030	26	26	28	28	28	30	30	30	32	32	32	34	36	38	38	40	42	42	44	46	46	48	50	52	54	54	56	56
	031	26	26	28	28	28	30	30	30	32	32	34	34	36	38	38	40	42	42	44	44	46	48	50	50	52	54	56	56
	032	26	26	28	28	28	28	30	30	32	32	32	34	36	38	38	40	42	42	44	44	46	48	50	50	52	54	56	56
	033	24	26	28	28	28	28	30	30	30	32	32	34	36	38	38	40	42	42	44	44	46	48	50	50	52	54	56	56
	034	26	26	28	28	28	28	30	30	30	32	32	34	36	36	38	40	40	42	44	44	46	46	50	50	52	54	56	56
RHODE ISLAND	035	22	24	26	26	26	26	26	26	28	28	28	30	32	32	32	34	36	36	38	38	38	40	42	44	46	46	48	48
	036	22	24	24	24	24	26	26	26	26	28	28	30	32	32	32	34	34	36	36	38	38	40	42	44	44	46	48	48
	037	22	22	24	24	24	26	26	26	26	28	28	28	30	32	32	34	34	36	36	38	38	40	42	44	44	46	48	48
	038	22	22	24	24	24	24	26	26	28	28	28	28	30	30	32	32	34	34	36	36	38	38	42	42	44	46	46	46
	039	22	22	24	24	24	24	24	26	26	26	26	28	30	30	32	32	34	34	36	36	38	38	42	42	44	46	46	46
CONNECTICUT	040	28	28	30	30	30	32	32	34	34	34	36	38	42	42	44	46	48	48	50	52	54	56	60	62	64	68	68	68
	041	28	28	30	30	30	32	32	34	34	34	36	38	40	42	44	46	48	48	50	52	54	56	60	62	64	68	68	68
	042	26	28	30	30	30	32	32	32	34	34	36	36	40	42	44	46	48	48	50	52	54	54	60	62	64	66	68	68
	043	26	28	30	30	30	30	32	32	34	34	36	36	40	42	42	44	46	48	50	52	54	54	60	62	64	66	68	68
	044	26	28	30	30	30	32	32	32	34	34	36	36	40	42	44	44	46	48	50	52	54	54	60	62	64	66	68	68
	045	26	28	30	30	30	32	32	32	34	34	36	36	40	42	44	44	46	48	50	52	54	54	60	62	64	66	68	68
	046	26	28	30	30	30	30	32	32	34	34	36	36	40	40	42	44	44	48	50	52	52	54	58	60	64	66	68	68
	047	26	28	30	30	30	32	32	32	34	34	36	38	40	40	42	44	46	48	48	50	52	54	58	60	64	66	68	68
	048	26	26	28	28	28	30	30	32	32	34	34	36	38	40	42	42	46	46	50	50	52	54	58	60	62	66	66	66
	049	26	26	28	28	28	30	30	32	32	34	34	36	38	40	42	42	46	46	48	50	52	54	58	60	62	66	66	66
NEW YORK	050	28	28	30	30	30	32	32	34	34	34	36	36	38	40	42	42	44	46	46	48	50	50	54	54	56	60	60	62

CONTINUED...

Geographical and Chronological Social Security Numbers

STATE OR POSSESSION	AREA	YEAR																											
		51	52	53	54	55	56	57	58	59	60	61	62	63	64	65	66	67	68	69	70	71	72	73	74	75	76	77	78
NEW YORK	051	28	28	30	30	30	32	32	34	34	34	36	36	40	40	42	42	44	46	46	48	50	50	54	54	56	60	60	62
	052	28	28	30	30	30	32	32	34	34	34	36	36	40	40	42	42	44	46	46	48	50	50	54	54	56	60	60	62
	053	28	28	30	30	30	32	32	34	34	34	36	36	38	40	42	42	44	46	46	48	50	50	54	54	56	60	60	62
	054	28	28	30	30	30	32	32	34	34	34	36	36	38	40	42	42	44	46	46	48	50	50	54	54	56	60	60	62
	055	28	28	30	30	30	32	32	34	34	34	36	36	38	40	42	42	44	46	46	48	50	50	54	54	56	60	60	62
	056	28	28	30	30	30	32	32	34	34	34	36	36	38	40	42	42	44	46	46	48	50	50	54	54	56	58	60	62
	057	28	28	30	30	30	32	32	34	34	34	36	36	38	40	42	42	44	46	46	48	50	50	54	54	56	58	60	62
	058	28	28	30	30	30	32	32	34	34	34	36	36	38	40	42	42	44	44	46	48	50	50	54	##	56	58	60	62
	059	28	28	30	30	30	32	32	34	34	34	36	36	38	40	42	42	44	46	46	48	50	50	54	54	56	58	60	62
	060	28	28	30	30	30	32	32	34	34	34	36	36	38	40	42	42	44	46	46	48	50	50	54	54	56	58	60	62
	061	28	28	30	30	30	32	32	34	34	34	36	36	36	38	42	42	44	46	46	48	50	50	54	54	56	58	60	62
	062	28	28	30	30	30	32	32	34	34	34	36	36	38	40	42	42	44	46	46	48	50	50	54	54	56	58	60	62
	063	28	28	30	30	30	32	32	34	34	34	36	36	38	40	42	42	44	46	46	48	50	50	54	54	56	##	60	62
	064	28	28	30	30	30	32	32	34	34	34	36	36	38	40	42	42	44	46	46	48	50	50	52	54	56	58	60	62
	065	28	28	30	30	30	32	32	34	34	34	36	36	38	40	40	42	44	44	46	48	50	50	52	54	56	58	60	62
	066	28	28	30	30	30	32	32	34	34	34	36	36	38	40	42	42	44	44	46	48	50	50	52	54	56	58	60	62
	067	28	28	30	30	30	32	32	34	34	34	36	36	38	40	42	42	44	44	46	48	50	50	52	54	56	58	60	62
	068	26	28	30	30	30	32	32	34	34	34	36	36	38	40	40	42	44	44	46	48	50	50	52	54	56	58	60	62
	069	28	28	28	30	30	32	32	34	34	34	36	36	38	40	42	42	44	46	46	48	50	50	52	54	56	58	60	62
	070	28	28	30	30	30	32	32	34	34	34	36	36	38	40	40	42	44	44	46	48	50	50	52	54	56	58	60	62
	071	28	28	28	30	30	32	32	34	34	34	36	36	38	40	40	42	44	44	46	48	50	50	52	54	56	58	60	62
	072	28	28	28	30	30	32	32	34	34	34	36	36	38	40	40	42	44	44	46	48	50	50	52	54	56	58	60	62
	073	28	28	28	30	30	32	32	34	34	34	36	36	38	40	40	42	44	46	46	48	50	50	52	54	56	58	60	62
	074	28	28	28	30	30	32	32	34	34	34	36	36	38	40	40	42	44	44	46	48	50	50	52	54	56	58	60	62
	075	28	28	28	30	30	32	32	34	34	34	36	36	38	40	40	42	44	44	46	48	50	50	52	54	56	58	60	62

CONTINUED...

Geographical and Chronological Social Security Numbers

STATE OR POSSESSION	AREA	YEAR																											
		51	52	53	54	55	56	57	58	59	60	61	62	63	64	65	66	67	68	69	70	71	72	73	74	75	76	77	78
NEW YORK	076	28	28	28	30	30	32	32	32	34	34	36	36	38	40	40	42	44	46	46	48	50	52	52	54	56	58	60	62
	077	26	28	28	30	30	32	32	32	34	34	34	36	38	40	40	42	44	44	46	48	50	52	52	54	56	58	60	62
	078	26	28	28	30	30	32	32	32	34	34	34	36	38	40	40	42	44	44	46	48	50	52	52	54	56	58	60	62
	079	28	28	28	30	30	32	32	32	34	34	34	36	38	40	40	42	44	44	46	48	50	52	52	54	56	58	60	62
	080	26	28	28	30	30	32	32	32	34	34	34	36	38	40	40	42	44	44	46	48	50	52	52	54	56	58	60	62
	081	28	28	28	30	30	32	32	32	34	34	34	36	38	40	40	42	44	44	46	48	50	52	52	54	56	58	60	62
	082	26	28	28	30	30	32	32	32	34	34	36	36	38	40	40	42	44	44	46	48	50	52	52	54	56	58	60	62
	083	26	28	28	30	30	32	32	32	34	34	36	36	38	40	40	42	44	44	46	48	50	52	52	54	56	58	60	60
	084	26	28	28	30	30	32	32	32	34	34	34	36	38	40	40	42	44	44	46	48	50	52	52	54	56	58	60	60
	085	26	28	28	30	30	32	32	32	34	34	34	36	38	40	40	42	44	44	46	48	50	52	52	54	56	58	60	60
	086	28	28	28	30	30	30	32	32	34	34	34	36	38	40	40	42	44	44	46	48	50	52	52	54	56	58	60	60
	087	28	28	28	30	30	30	32	32	34	34	34	36	38	40	40	42	44	44	46	48	50	52	52	54	56	58	60	60
	088	28	28	28	30	30	30	32	32	34	34	34	36	38	40	40	42	44	44	46	48	50	52	52	54	56	58	60	60
	089	26	28	28	30	30	30	32	32	34	34	34	36	38	40	40	42	44	44	46	48	50	52	52	54	56	58	60	60
	090	28	28	28	30	30	30	32	32	34	34	34	36	38	40	40	42	44	44	46	48	50	52	52	54	56	58	60	60
	091	26	28	28	30	30	30	32	32	34	34	34	36	38	40	40	42	44	44	46	48	50	52	52	54	56	58	60	60
	092	26	28	28	30	30	30	32	32	34	34	34	36	38	40	40	42	44	44	46	48	50	52	52	54	56	58	60	60
	093	26	28	28	30	30	30	32	32	34	34	34	36	38	40	40	42	44	44	46	48	50	52	52	54	56	58	60	60
	094	26	28	28	30	30	30	32	32	34	34	34	36	38	38	40	42	44	44	46	48	50	52	52	54	56	58	60	60
	095	26	28	28	30	30	30	32	32	34	34	34	36	38	40	40	42	44	44	46	48	50	52	52	54	56	58	60	60
	096	26	28	28	30	30	30	32	32	34	34	34	36	38	38	40	42	42	44	46	48	50	52	52	54	56	58	60	60
	097	26	28	28	30	30	30	32	32	34	34	34	36	38	40	40	42	44	44	46	48	50	52	52	54	56	58	60	60
	098	26	28	28	30	30	30	32	32	32	34	34	36	38	38	40	42	42	44	46	48	50	52	52	54	56	58	60	60
	099	26	28	28	30	30	30	32	32	34	34	34	36	38	38	40	42	42	44	46	48	50	52	52	54	56	58	60	60
	100	26	28	28	30	30	30	32	32	32	34	34	36	38	38	40	42	42	44	46	48	50	52	52	54	56	58	60	60

CONTINUED...

Geographical and Chronological Social Security Numbers

YEAR

STATE OR POSSESSION	AREA	51	52	53	54	55	56	57	58	59	60	61	62	63	64	65	66	67	68	69	70	71	72	73	74	75	76	77	78
NEW YORK	101	26	28	28	30	30	30	32	32	32	34	34	36	38	38	40	40	42	44	46	46	48	50	52	54	56	58	60	60
	102	26	28	28	28	30	30	32	32	32	34	34	36	38	38	40	40	42	44	46	48	48	50	52	54	56	58	60	60
	103	26	28	28	28	30	30	32	32	32	34	34	36	38	38	40	40	42	44	46	48	48	50	52	54	56	58	60	60
	104	26	28	28	28	30	30	32	32	32	34	34	36	38	38	40	40	42	44	46	48	48	50	52	54	56	58	60	60
	105	26	28	28	28	30	30	32	32	32	34	34	36	38	38	40	40	42	44	46	48	48	50	52	54	56	58	60	60
	106	26	28	28	28	30	30	32	32	32	34	34	36	38	38	40	40	42	44	46	46	48	50	52	54	56	58	60	60
	107	26	28	28	28	30	30	32	32	32	34	34	36	38	38	40	40	42	44	46	46	48	50	52	54	56	58	60	60
	108	26	28	28	28	30	30	32	32	32	34	34	36	38	38	40	40	42	44	46	46	48	50	52	54	56	58	60	60
	109	26	28	28	28	30	30	32	32	32	34	34	36	38	38	40	40	42	44	46	46	48	50	52	54	56	58	60	60
	110	26	28	28	28	30	30	32	32	32	34	34	36	38	38	40	40	42	44	46	46	48	50	52	54	56	58	60	60
	111	26	28	28	28	30	30	32	32	32	34	34	36	38	38	40	40	42	44	46	46	48	50	52	54	56	58	60	60
	112	26	28	28	28	30	30	32	32	32	34	34	36	38	38	40	40	42	44	46	48	48	50	52	54	56	58	60	60
	113	26	28	28	28	30	30	30	32	32	34	34	36	38	38	40	40	42	44	46	46	48	50	52	54	56	58	60	60
	114	26	28	28	28	30	30	32	32	32	34	34	36	38	38	40	40	42	44	46	48	48	50	52	54	56	58	60	60
	115	26	28	28	28	30	30	30	32	32	34	34	36	38	38	40	40	42	44	46	48	48	50	52	54	56	58	60	60
	116	26	28	28	28	30	30	32	32	32	34	34	36	38	38	40	40	42	44	46	46	48	50	52	54	56	58	60	60
	117	26	28	28	28	30	30	32	32	34	34	34	36	38	38	40	40	42	44	46	46	48	50	52	54	56	58	60	60
	118	26	28	28	28	30	30	32	32	32	34	34	36	38	38	40	40	42	44	46	48	48	50	52	54	56	58	60	60
	119	26	28	28	28	30	30	32	32	32	34	34	36	36	38	40	40	42	44	46	46	48	50	52	54	56	58	60	60
	120	26	28	28	28	30	30	32	32	32	34	34	36	38	38	40	40	42	44	46	46	48	50	52	54	56	58	60	60
	121	26	28	28	28	30	30	32	32	32	34	34	36	36	38	40	42	42	44	46	46	48	50	52	54	56	58	60	60
	122	26	26	28	28	30	30	32	32	32	34	34	36	38	38	40	40	42	44	46	46	48	50	52	54	56	58	58	60
	123	26	26	28	28	30	30	30	32	32	34	34	36	36	38	40	42	42	44	46	46	48	50	52	54	56	58	58	60
	124	26	26	28	28	30	30	32	32	32	34	34	36	38	38	40	40	42	44	46	46	48	50	52	54	56	58	58	58
	125	26	26	28	28	30	30	32	32	32	34	34	34	38	38	40	40	42	44	46	48	48	50	52	54	56	58	58	58

Geographical and Chronological Social Security Numbers

YEAR

STATE OR POSSESSION	AREA	51	52	53	54	55	56	57	58	59	60	61	62	63	64	65	66	67	68	69	70	71	72	73	74	75	76	77	78
NEW YORK (CONTINUED)	126	26	26	28	28	30	30	30	32	32	34	34	34	38	38	40	40	42	44	44	46	50	52	54	54	54	58	58	60
	127	26	26	28	28	30	30	30	32	32	34	34	34	38	38	40	40	42	44	46	46	50	52	54	54	54	58	58	60
	128	26	26	28	28	30	30	30	32	32	34	34	34	38	40	40	40	42	44	44	46	50	52	54	54	54	58	58	60
	129	26	26	28	28	30	30	30	32	32	34	34	34	38	38	40	40	42	44	46	46	50	52	54	54	54	58	58	60
	130	26	26	28	28	30	30	30	32	32	34	34	34	38	38	40	40	42	44	44	46	50	52	52	52	54	58	58	60
	131	26	26	28	28	30	30	30	32	32	34	34	34	36	38	40	40	42	44	46	46	50	52	52	52	54	58	58	60
	132	26	26	28	28	30	30	30	32	32	32	34	34	38	38	40	40	42	44	44	46	50	52	52	52	54	58	58	60
	133	26	26	28	28	30	30	30	32	32	32	34	36	38	38	40	40	42	44	46	46	50	52	52	52	54	58	58	60
	134	26	26	28	28	30	30	30	32	34	34	34	34	36	38	40	40	42	44	44	46	48	52	52	52	54	58	58	60
NEW JERSEY	135	26	28	28	30	30	32	32	32	32	32	36	36	38	40	42	44	46	46	48	50	52	56	58	58	62	64	66	68
	136	26	28	28	30	30	32	32	32	34	34	36	36	38	40	42	44	46	46	48	50	52	56	58	58	62	64	66	68
	137	26	28	28	30	30	30	32	32	34	34	36	36	40	40	42	44	46	46	48	50	52	56	58	58	62	64	66	68
	138	26	28	28	30	30	30	32	32	34	34	36	36	38	40	42	44	46	46	48	50	52	56	58	58	62	64	66	68
	139	26	28	28	28	30	30	32	32	34	34	36	36	38	40	42	44	46	46	48	50	52	56	58	58	62	64	66	68
	140	26	28	28	28	30	30	32	32	34	34	34	36	38	40	42	44	46	46	48	50	52	56	58	58	60	64	66	68
	141	26	28	28	28	30	30	32	32	34	34	36	36	38	40	42	44	46	46	48	50	52	56	58	58	60	64	66	68
	142	26	28	28	28	30	30	32	32	34	34	34	36	38	40	42	44	44	46	48	50	52	56	58	58	60	64	66	66
	143	26	28	28	28	30	30	32	32	32	34	34	36	38	40	42	44	44	46	48	50	52	56	58	58	60	64	66	66
	144	26	28	28	28	30	30	32	32	32	34	34	36	38	40	42	44	44	46	48	50	52	56	58	58	60	64	66	66
	145	26	26	28	28	30	30	32	32	32	34	34	36	38	40	42	44	44	46	48	50	52	56	58	58	60	64	66	66
	146	26	26	28	28	30	30	32	32	32	34	34	36	38	40	42	42	44	46	48	50	52	56	58	58	60	64	66	66
	147	26	26	28	28	30	30	32	32	32	34	34	36	38	40	40	42	44	46	48	48	52	56	58	58	60	64	66	66
	148	26	26	28	28	30	30	30	32	32	34	34	36	38	40	40	42	44	46	48	50	52	56	58	58	60	62	66	66
	149	26	26	28	28	30	30	30	32	32	34	34	36	38	40	40	42	44	46	48	48	52	56	58	58	60	62	66	66
	150	26	26	28	28	30	30	30	32	32	34	34	36	38	40	40	42	44	46	48	48	52	56	58	58	60	62	66	66

CONTINUED...

Geographical and Chronological Social Security Numbers

YEAR

STATE OR POSSESSION	AREA	51	52	53	54	55	56	57	58	59	60	61	62	63	64	65	66	67	68	69	70	71	72	73	74	75	76	77	78
NEW JERSEY	151	26	26	28	28	28	30	30	32	32	34	34	36	38	38	40	42	44	46	46	48	50	52	56	58	60	62	64	66
	152	26	26	28	28	28	30	30	32	32	34	34	36	38	38	40	42	44	46	46	48	50	52	56	58	60	62	64	66
	153	26	26	28	28	28	30	30	32	32	32	34	34	38	38	40	42	44	46	48	48	50	52	54	54	60	62	64	66
	154	24	26	26	28	28	30	30	32	32	32	34	34	38	38	40	42	44	46	48	48	50	52	54	58	60	62	64	66
	155	24	26	26	28	28	30	30	32	32	32	34	36	38	38	40	42	44	46	46	48	50	52	54	58	60	62	64	66
	156	26	26	26	28	28	30	30	32	32	32	34	34	38	38	40	42	44	46	46	48	50	52	54	58	60	62	64	66
	157	26	26	26	28	28	30	30	30	32	32	34	34	38	38	40	42	44	44	48	48	50	52	54	58	60	62	64	66
	158	26	26	26	28	28	30	30	30	32	32	34	34	36	38	40	42	44	44	46	48	50	52	54	56	60	62	64	66
PENNSYLVANIA	159	28	28	30	30	30	32	32	34	34	34	36	36	38	40	40	42	44	44	46	46	48	48	52	52	54	56	58	58
	160	28	28	30	30	30	32	32	34	34	34	36	36	38	40	40	42	44	44	46	46	48	48	52	52	54	56	58	58
	161	28	28	30	30	30	32	32	34	34	34	36	36	38	40	40	42	42	44	46	46	48	48	52	52	54	56	58	58
	162	28	28	30	30	30	32	32	34	34	34	36	36	38	40	40	42	42	44	46	46	48	48	52	52	54	56	58	58
	163	28	28	30	30	30	32	32	34	34	34	36	36	38	40	40	42	42	44	46	46	48	48	52	52	54	56	58	58
	164	28	28	30	30	30	32	32	34	34	34	36	36	38	40	40	42	42	44	46	46	48	48	52	52	54	56	58	58
	165	28	28	30	30	30	32	32	32	34	34	34	36	38	38	40	42	42	44	46	46	48	48	52	52	54	56	58	58
	166	28	28	30	30	30	32	32	32	34	34	36	36	38	38	40	42	42	44	46	46	48	48	52	52	54	56	58	58
	167	28	28	30	30	30	32	32	32	34	34	36	36	38	38	40	42	42	44	46	46	48	48	52	52	54	56	58	58
	168	28	28	30	30	30	32	32	32	34	34	36	36	38	38	40	42	42	44	46	46	48	48	52	52	54	56	58	58
	169	28	28	30	30	30	32	32	32	34	34	36	36	38	38	40	42	42	44	46	46	48	48	52	52	54	56	56	58
	170	28	28	30	30	30	32	32	32	34	34	34	36	38	38	40	42	42	44	46	46	48	48	52	52	54	56	58	58
	171	28	28	30	30	30	32	32	32	34	34	34	36	38	38	40	42	42	44	46	46	48	48	52	52	54	56	58	58
	172	28	28	28	30	30	32	32	32	34	34	34	36	38	38	40	42	42	44	46	46	48	48	50	52	54	56	58	58
	173	28	28	28	30	30	32	32	32	34	34	34	36	38	38	40	42	42	44	44	46	48	48	50	52	54	56	58	58
	174	28	28	28	30	30	32	32	32	34	34	34	36	38	38	40	42	42	44	44	46	48	48	50	52	54	56	58	58
	175	28	28	28	30	30	32	32	32	34	34	34	36	38	38	40	42	42	44	44	46	48	48	50	52	54	56	58	58

CONTINUED...

Geographical and Chronological Social Security Numbers

STATE OR POSSESSION	AREA	YEAR																											
		51	52	53	54	55	56	57	58	59	60	61	62	63	64	65	66	67	68	69	70	71	72	73	74	75	76	77	78
PENNSYLVANIA	176	28	28	28	30	30	32	32	32	34	34	34	36	38	38	40	42	42	44	46	46	48	48	50	52	54	56	58	58
	177	26	28	28	30	30	30	32	32	34	34	34	36	38	38	40	42	42	44	44	46	46	48	50	52	54	56	58	58
	178	26	28	28	30	30	30	32	32	34	34	34	36	38	38	40	42	42	44	46	46	48	48	50	52	54	56	58	58
	179	26	28	28	30	30	30	32	32	34	34	34	36	38	38	40	42	42	44	46	46	48	48	50	52	54	56	58	58
	180	26	28	28	30	30	32	32	32	34	34	34	36	38	38	40	42	42	44	46	46	48	48	50	52	54	56	58	58
	181	28	28	28	30	30	32	32	32	34	34	34	36	38	38	40	42	42	44	44	46	46	48	50	52	54	56	58	58
	182	28	28	28	30	30	30	32	32	34	34	34	36	38	38	40	40	42	44	44	46	46	48	50	52	54	56	58	58
	183	26	28	28	30	30	30	32	32	32	34	34	36	38	38	40	40	42	44	44	46	46	48	50	52	54	56	58	58
	184	26	28	28	30	30	30	32	32	34	34	34	36	38	38	40	42	42	44	44	46	46	48	50	52	54	56	58	58
	185	26	28	28	30	30	30	32	32	32	34	34	36	38	38	40	40	42	44	44	46	46	48	50	52	54	56	58	58
	186	26	28	28	30	30	30	32	32	32	34	34	36	38	38	40	40	42	44	44	46	46	48	50	52	54	56	58	58
	187	26	28	28	28	30	30	32	32	32	34	34	36	38	38	40	40	42	42	44	46	46	48	50	52	54	56	58	58
	188	26	28	28	30	30	30	32	32	32	34	34	36	38	38	40	40	42	44	44	46	46	48	50	52	54	56	58	58
	189	26	28	28	28	30	30	32	32	32	34	34	34	36	38	40	40	42	44	44	46	46	48	50	52	54	56	58	58
	190	26	28	28	28	30	30	32	32	32	34	34	36	36	38	40	40	42	42	44	46	46	48	50	52	54	56	58	58
	191	26	28	28	28	30	30	32	32	32	34	34	34	36	38	40	40	42	44	44	46	46	48	50	52	54	56	58	58
	192	26	28	28	28	30	30	32	32	32	34	34	34	38	38	40	40	42	42	44	46	46	48	50	52	54	56	58	58
	193	26	28	28	28	30	30	32	32	32	34	34	34	36	38	40	40	42	42	44	46	46	48	50	52	54	56	58	58
	194	26	28	28	28	30	30	32	32	32	34	34	34	36	38	40	40	42	42	44	46	46	48	50	52	54	56	58	58
	195	26	28	28	28	30	30	32	32	32	34	34	34	38	38	40	40	42	42	44	46	46	48	50	52	54	56	58	58
	196	26	28	28	28	30	30	32	32	32	34	34	34	36	38	38	40	42	42	44	46	46	48	50	52	54	56	58	58
	197	26	28	28	28	30	30	32	32	32	34	34	34	36	38	38	40	42	42	44	46	46	48	50	52	54	56	58	58
	198	26	28	28	28	30	30	32	32	32	34	34	34	38	38	38	40	42	42	44	46	46	48	50	52	54	56	58	58
	199	26	28	28	28	30	30	32	32	32	34	34	34	36	38	38	40	42	42	44	46	46	48	50	52	54	56	58	58
	200	26	28	28	28	30	30	32	32	32	32	34	34	36	38	38	40	42	42	44	46	46	48	50	52	54	56	58	58

CONTINUED....

Geographical and Chronological Social Security Numbers

YEAR

STATE OR POSSESSION	AREA	51	52	53	54	55	56	57	58	59	60	61	62	63	64	65	66	67	68	69	70	71	72	73	74	75	76	77	78
PENNSYLVANIA (CONTINUED)	201	26	28	28	28	30	30	32	32	32	34	34	34	36	38	40	40	42	42	44	46	46	48	50	52	54	56	56	58
	202	26	28	28	28	30	30	30	32	32	32	34	34	36	38	38	40	42	42	44	44	46	48	50	52	54	56	56	58
	203	26	28	28	28	30	30	32	32	32	32	34	34	36	38	38	40	42	42	44	44	46	48	50	52	54	56	56	58
	204	26	26	28	28	30	30	30	32	32	32	34	34	36	38	38	40	42	42	44	44	46	46	50	52	54	54	56	58
	205	26	26	28	28	30	30	30	32	32	32	34	34	36	38	38	40	42	42	44	46	46	46	50	52	54	54	56	58
	206	26	26	28	28	30	30	30	32	32	32	34	34	36	38	38	40	42	42	44	44	46	46	50	52	54	54	56	56
	207	26	28	28	28	30	30	30	32	32	32	34	34	36	38	38	40	42	42	44	44	46	46	50	52	54	54	56	56
	208	26	26	28	28	30	30	30	32	32	32	34	34	38	38	38	40	42	42	44	44	46	46	50	52	54	54	56	56
	209	26	26	28	28	30	30	30	32	32	32	34	34	36	38	38	40	42	42	44	44	46	46	50	52	54	54	56	56
	210	26	26	28	28	28	30	30	32	32	32	34	34	36	38	38	40	42	42	44	44	46	46	50	52	54	54	56	56
	211	26	26	28	28	28	30	30	32	32	32	34	34	36	38	38	40	42	42	44	44	46	46	50	52	54	54	56	56
MARYLAND	212	32	34	34	36	36	38	40	40	42	42	44	46	50	52	54	56	58	62	64	66	70	72	76	80	82	86	90	92
	213	32	34	34	34	36	38	38	40	42	42	44	46	50	52	54	56	60	62	64	68	70	72	76	80	82	86	90	92
	214	32	34	34	34	36	38	38	40	40	42	44	46	50	52	54	56	58	60	64	66	70	72	76	80	82	86	90	90
	215	32	32	34	34	36	38	38	40	40	42	44	46	50	50	54	56	58	60	64	66	70	72	76	80	82	86	88	90
	216	32	32	34	34	36	38	38	40	40	42	44	46	48	50	54	56	58	60	64	66	70	72	76	78	82	86	88	90
	217	32	32	34	34	36	38	38	38	40	42	44	44	48	50	52	56	58	62	64	66	70	72	76	78	82	86	88	90
	218	32	32	34	34	36	36	38	40	40	42	42	44	48	50	52	56	58	60	64	66	70	72	76	78	82	86	88	90
	219	30	32	32	34	34	36	38	38	40	42	42	44	48	50	52	56	58	60	62	66	68	72	76	78	82	86	88	90
	220	30	32	32	34	34	36	38	38	40	40	42	44	48	50	52	56	58	60	62	66	68	72	74	78	80	84	88	90
DELAWARE	221	22	22	22	24	24	26	26	26	28	28	30	30	32	32	34	36	38	40	40	42	44	46	52	54	58	60	60	60
	222	20	20	22	22	24	24	24	26	26	26	28	28	30	32	34	34	36	38	40	42	44	46	52	54	56	58	60	60
VERMONT	223	42	44	46	48	50	52	54	54	56	58	60	62	66	68	70	74	76	80	82	86	88	90	96	02	06	11	15	17
	224	40	44	46	48	50	52	52	54	56	58	60	62	66	68	70	74	76	80	82	84	88	90	96	02	06	11	15	17
	225	40	44	46	46	48	52	52	54	56	58	58	60	66	68	70	74	76	80	82	84	88	90	96	02	06	11	13	17

CONTINUED...

Geographical and Chronological Social Security Numbers

STATE OR POSSESSION	AREA	51	52	53	54	55	56	57	58	59	60	61	62	63	64	65	66	67	68	69	70	71	72	73	74	75	76	77	78
VIRGINIA	226	42	44	46	46	48	50	52	54	56	56	58	60	66	68	70	74	76	80	82	84	88	90	96	02	06	11	13	17
	227	42	44	46	46	48	50	52	54	54	56	58	60	64	68	70	74	76	78	82	84	88	90	96	02	06	11	13	15
	228	42	44	46	46	48	50	52	54	54	56	58	60	64	68	70	74	76	78	82	84	86	90	96	02	06	11	13	15
	229	42	42	44	46	48	50	52	54	54	56	58	60	64	66	70	72	76	78	82	84	86	90	96	02	04	08	13	15
	230	42	42	44	46	48	50	52	52	54	56	58	60	64	66	70	72	76	78	80	84	86	90	94	02	04	08	13	15
	231	40	42	44	46	48	50	52	52	54	56	58	60	64	66	70	72	74	78	80	84	86	88	02	98	04	08	13	15
W. VIRGINIA & N. CAROLINA	232	54	56	58	58	60	62	64	66	68	70	70	72	76	78	80	82	84	86	88	92	92	94	02	04	06	11	13	15
W. VIRGINIA	233	54	54	56	58	60	62	64	66	68	70	70	72	74	76	80	82	84	86	88	90	92	94	98	04	06	11	13	15
	234	52	54	56	58	60	62	64	66	68	70	70	72	74	76	80	82	84	86	88	90	92	94	98	04	06	11	13	15
	235	52	54	56	58	60	62	64	66	68	70	70	72	74	76	78	82	84	86	88	90	92	94	98	02	06	08	13	13
	236	52	54	56	58	60	62	62	66	68	70	68	70	74	76	78	80	84	86	88	90	92	94	98	02	06	08	11	13
N. CAROLINA	237	50	52	54	56	58	60	62	66	66	70	72	74	76	80	82	86	90	92	94	98	02	04	11	15	19	23	27	29
	238	50	52	54	56	58	60	62	64	66	68	70	74	78	80	82	86	90	92	94	98	02	04	11	15	19	23	27	29
	239	48	52	54	54	58	60	62	64	66	68	70	72	76	80	82	86	90	92	94	98	02	04	11	15	19	23	25	29
	240	50	50	54	54	58	60	62	64	66	68	70	72	78	80	82	86	88	90	94	98	02	04	11	15	19	23	25	27
	241	48	50	52	54	56	60	62	64	66	68	70	72	76	78	82	86	88	92	94	98	02	04	11	15	19	23	25	27
	242	50	52	54	54	58	60	62	64	66	68	70	72	76	78	82	86	88	92	94	96	02	04	11	15	19	23	25	27
	243	48	50	52	54	56	60	62	64	66	68	70	72	76	78	82	86	88	90	94	96	02	04	11	15	19	23	25	27
	244	48	50	52	54	56	60	62	64	66	68	70	72	76	78	82	86	88	90	94	96	02	04	11	15	17	21	25	27
	245	48	50	52	54	56	60	62	64	66	68	70	72	76	78	82	84	88	90	92	96	02	04	11	15	17	21	25	27
	246	48	50	52	54	56	58	62	64	66	68	70	72	76	78	82	84	88	90	92	96	02	04	11	15	17	21	25	27
S. CAROLINA	247	54	52	58	58	62	64	66	68	70	74	76	78	82	84	88	94	96	98	04	06	11	13	19	25	31	33	37	39
	248	54	52	56	58	62	64	66	68	70	72	76	78	82	84	88	94	96	98	04	06	11	13	19	25	29	33	37	39
	249	52	52	56	58	62	64	66	68	70	72	74	78	82	84	88	92	96	98	02	06	08	13	19	25	29	33	37	39
	250	52	52	56	58	60	64	66	68	70	72	74	78	82	84	88	92	94	98	02	06	08	13	19	25	29	33	35	39

YEAR

CONTINUED....

Geographical and Chronological Social Security Numbers

STATE OR POSSESSION	AREA	51	52	53	54	55	56	57	58	59	60	61	62	63	64	65	66	67	68	69	70	71	72	73	74	75	76	77	78
S. CAROLINA	251	52	54	56	58	60	64	66	68	70	72	74	76	82	84	88	94	94	96	02	06	08	13	19	25	29	33	35	39
GEORGIA	252	52	54	56	56	58	60	64	64	66	68	70	72	76	78	82	88	88	92	94	98	02	06	13	19	23	27	29	31
	253	52	54	56	56	58	60	62	64	66	68	70	72	76	78	82	88	88	92	94	96	02	06	15	19	23	27	29	31
	254	50	52	54	56	58	60	62	64	66	68	70	72	76	78	82	88	88	92	94	98	02	04	15	19	23	27	29	31
	255	52	52	54	56	58	60	62	64	66	68	70	72	76	78	82	88	88	92	94	96	02	04	15	19	23	27	29	31
	256	52	52	54	56	58	60	62	64	66	68	68	70	74	78	80	88	88	90	94	96	02	04	15	17	21	27	29	31
	257	52	52	54	56	58	60	62	64	64	66	68	70	74	76	80	88	88	90	94	96	02	04	15	17	21	27	29	31
	258	50	52	54	56	58	60	62	62	64	66	68	70	74	76	80	88	88	90	94	96	02	04	15	17	21	27	29	29
	259	50	52	54	56	58	60	62	62	64	66	68	70	74	76	80	84	86	90	92	96	02	04	15	17	21	25	27	29
	260	50	52	54	54	56	60	62	62	64	66	68	70	74	76	80	86	86	90	92	96	02	04	51	17	21	25	27	29
FLORIDA	261	48	50	52	54	58	60	62	64	68	70	74	78	88	94	98	13	13	19	23	31	35	39	50	61	67	75	81	87
	262	50	50	52	54	58	60	62	64	66	70	72	80	86	94	98	13	13	19	23	29	35	39	51	59	67	75	81	87
	263	48	50	52	54	56	60	62	64	66	70	72	78	88	92	98	13	13	17	23	29	35	39	51	59	67	75	81	85
	264	48	50	52	54	56	60	62	64	66	70	72	78	86	90	98	13	13	17	23	29	35	39	51	59	67	75	81	85
	265	48	50	52	54	56	60	62	64	66	68	72	76	86	92	98	13	13	17	23	29	35	39	51	59	67	73	81	85
	266	48	50	52	52	56	60	62	64	66	70	72	76	86	92	98	13	13	17	23	29	35	39	51	59	67	73	81	85
	267	48	50	50	54	56	58	60	62	66	68	72	76	84	92	98	11	11	17	23	29	33	39	49	59	67	73	79	85
OHIO	268	30	32	32	34	34	36	36	38	38	40	40	42	44	46	50	52	52	54	56	58	58	60	64	66	68	72	72	74
	269	30	32	32	34	34	36	36	38	38	40	40	42	44	46	50	52	52	54	54	56	58	60	64	66	68	72	72	74
	270	30	32	32	34	34	36	36	38	38	40	40	40	44	46	50	52	52	54	54	56	58	60	64	66	68	72	72	74
	271	30	32	32	34	34	36	36	38	38	38	40	40	44	46	50	52	52	54	54	56	58	60	64	66	68	72	72	74
	272	30	32	32	34	34	36	36	38	38	38	40	40	44	46	50	52	52	54	56	56	58	60	64	66	68	72	72	74
	273	30	32	32	34	34	36	36	36	38	38	40	40	44	46	50	52	52	54	54	56	58	60	64	66	68	72	72	74
	274	30	32	32	34	34	36	36	38	38	38	40	40	44	46	50	52	52	54	54	56	58	60	64	66	68	70	70	74
	275	30	32	32	34	34	36	36	36	38	38	40	40	44	46	50	52	52	52	54	56	58	60	64	66	68	70	70	74

CONTINUED...

Geographical and Chronological Social Security Numbers

YEAR

STATE OR POSSESSION / AREA	51	52	53	54	55	56	57	58	59	60	61	62	63	64	65	66	67	68	69	70	71	72	73	74	75	76	77	78
OHIO (CONTINUED) 276	30	32	32	34	34	36	36	36	38	38	40	40	44	46	48	50	52	52	54	56	58	60	64	66	68	70	72	74
277	30	32	32	32	34	36	36	36	38	38	40	40	44	46	48	50	52	52	54	56	58	60	64	66	68	70	72	74
278	30	32	32	32	34	36	36	36	38	38	40	40	44	46	48	50	50	54	54	56	58	60	64	66	68	70	72	72
279	30	32	32	32	34	34	36	36	38	38	40	40	44	46	48	50	50	52	56	56	58	60	64	66	68	70	72	72
280	30	32	32	32	34	36	36	36	38	38	40	40	44	46	48	50	50	52	54	56	58	60	64	66	68	70	72	72
281	30	32	32	32	34	36	36	36	38	38	40	40	44	46	48	50	50	52	54	56	58	60	64	66	68	70	72	72
282	30	32	32	32	34	34	36	36	38	38	40	40	48	46	46	50	50	52	54	56	58	60	64	66	68	70	72	72
283	30	30	32	32	34	34	36	36	38	38	40	40	48	46	48	50	50	52	54	56	58	60	64	66	68	70	72	72
284	30	30	32	32	34	34	36	36	38	38	40	40	48	46	48	50	50	52	54	56	58	58	64	66	68	70	72	72
285	30	30	32	32	34	34	36	36	38	38	38	40	48	46	46	50	50	52	54	56	58	58	64	66	68	70	72	72
286	30	30	32	32	34	34	36	36	38	38	40	40	48	46	46	48	50	52	54	56	58	58	64	66	68	70	72	72
287	30	30	32	32	34	34	36	36	38	38	38	40	48	46	46	48	50	52	54	56	58	58	64	66	68	70	72	72
288	30	30	32	32	34	34	36	36	36	38	38	40	48	44	46	48	50	52	54	56	58	58	64	66	68	70	72	72
289	30	30	32	32	34	34	36	36	38	38	38	40	48	44	48	48	50	52	54	56	58	58	64	66	68	70	72	72
290	30	30	32	32	34	34	36	36	36	38	38	40	48	44	48	48	50	52	54	56	58	58	64	66	68	70	72	72
291	30	30	32	32	34	34	36	36	36	38	38	40	48	44	48	48	50	52	54	56	56	58	64	66	68	70	72	72
292	30	30	32	32	34	34	36	36	36	38	38	40	42	44	48	48	50	52	54	56	58	58	62	66	68	70	72	72
293	30	30	32	32	34	34	36	36	36	38	38	40	44	44	48	48	50	52	54	56	56	58	62	64	68	70	72	72
294	30	30	32	32	32	34	34	36	36	38	38	40	42	44	48	48	50	52	54	56	58	58	62	64	68	70	72	72
295	28	30	32	32	34	34	34	36	36	38	38	40	44	44	48	48	50	52	54	56	56	58	62	64	68	70	72	72
296	28	30	32	32	32	34	34	36	36	38	38	40	44	44	48	48	50	52	54	56	56	58	62	64	68	70	70	72
297	28	30	32	32	32	34	34	36	36	38	38	42	42	44	48	48	50	52	54	56	56	58	62	64	68	70	70	72
298	28	30	32	32	32	34	34	36	36	38	38	40	44	44	48	48	50	52	54	56	56	58	62	64	66	70	70	72
299	28	30	32	32	32	34	36	36	36	38	38	40	44	44	48	48	50	52	54	56	56	58	62	64	66	70	70	72
300	30	30	30	32	32	34	36	36	38	38	40	44	44	44	48	48	50	52	54	54	56	58	62	66	66	70	70	72

CONTINUED...

Geographical and Chronological Social Security Numbers

STATE OR POSSESSION	AREA	51	52	53	54	55	56	57	58	59	60	61	62	63	64	65	66	67	68	69	70	71	72	73	74	75	76	77	78
OHIO	301	28	30	30	32	32	34	34	36	36	38	38	40	42	44	46	48	50	52	54	56	56	58	62	64	66	70	70	72
	302	28	30	30	32	32	34	34	36	36	38	38	40	42	44	46	48	50	52	54	56	56	58	62	64	66	70	70	72
INDIANA	303	36	36	38	38	40	42	42	44	44	46	46	48	52	52	54	48	58	60	62	64	66	68	72	74	76	80	82	82
	304	34	36	38	38	40	42	42	44	44	46	46	48	52	52	54	56	58	60	62	64	66	68	72	74	76	80	82	82
	305	34	36	38	38	40	42	42	44	44	46	46	48	52	52	54	56	58	60	62	64	66	68	72	74	76	80	80	82
	306	34	36	36	38	40	40	42	42	44	46	46	48	50	52	54	56	58	60	62	64	66	68	72	74	76	80	80	82
	307	36	36	36	38	40	40	42	42	44	44	46	48	50	52	54	56	58	60	62	64	66	68	72	74	76	78	80	82
	308	34	36	36	38	40	40	42	42	44	44	46	48	50	52	54	56	58	60	62	64	66	68	72	74	76	78	80	82
	309	34	36	36	38	38	40	42	42	44	44	46	48	50	52	54	56	58	60	62	64	66	68	72	74	76	78	80	82
	310	34	36	36	38	38	40	42	42	44	44	46	48	50	52	54	56	58	60	62	64	66	68	72	74	76	78	80	82
	311	34	36	36	36	38	40	42	42	44	44	46	46	50	52	54	56	58	58	62	64	66	68	70	74	76	78	80	82
	312	34	34	36	38	38	40	42	42	44	44	46	46	50	52	54	56	58	58	60	62	64	66	70	72	74	78	80	82
	313	34	34	36	36	38	40	42	42	44	44	46	46	50	52	54	56	58	58	60	62	64	66	70	72	74	78	80	82
	314	34	34	36	36	38	40	40	42	42	44	44	46	48	50	52	54	56	58	60	62	64	66	70	72	74	78	80	82
	315	34	34	36	36	38	38	40	42	42	44	44	46	50	50	52	56	56	58	60	62	64	66	70	72	74	78	80	80
	316	34	34	36	36	38	40	40	42	42	44	44	46	48	50	52	54	56	58	60	62	64	66	70	72	74	78	80	80
	317	34	34	36	36	38	40	40	42	42	44	44	46	48	50	52	54	56	58	60	62	64	66	70	72	74	78	80	80
ILLINOIS	318	28	30	30	32	32	34	34	34	36	36	38	38	40	42	44	46	46	48	50	52	54	54	58	60	62	64	66	66
	319	28	30	30	32	32	34	34	34	36	36	36	38	40	42	44	46	46	48	50	52	52	54	58	60	62	64	66	66
	320	28	30	30	30	32	34	34	34	36	36	38	38	40	42	44	44	46	48	50	52	52	54	58	60	62	66	66	66
	321	28	30	30	30	32	34	34	34	36	36	38	38	40	42	44	46	46	48	50	52	54	54	58	60	62	64	66	66
	322	28	30	30	30	32	32	34	34	36	36	38	38	40	42	44	44	46	48	50	52	54	54	58	60	62	64	66	66
	323	28	30	30	30	32	34	34	34	36	36	36	38	40	42	44	44	46	48	50	52	54	54	58	60	62	66	66	66
	324	28	30	30	30	32	34	34	34	36	36	36	38	40	42	44	44	46	48	50	52	52	54	58	60	62	64	64	66
	325	28	30	30	30	32	34	34	34	36	36	36	38	40	42	44	44	##	48	50	52	52	54	58	60	62	64	64	66

YEAR

CONTINUED...

Geographical and Chronological Social Security Numbers

YEAR

STATE OR POSSESSION	AREA	51	52	53	54	55	56	57	58	59	60	61	62	63	64	65	66	67	68	69	70	71	72	73	74	75	76	77	78
ILLINOIS	326	28	30	30	30	32	32	34	34	36	36	36	38	40	42	44	44	46	48	50	52	54	54	58	60	62	64	66	66
	327	28	30	30	30	32	32	34	34	36	36	36	38	40	42	44	44	46	48	50	52	54	54	58	60	62	64	64	66
	328	28	30	30	30	32	32	34	34	36	36	36	38	40	42	42	44	46	48	50	52	52	54	58	58	60	64	64	66
	329	28	28	30	30	32	32	34	34	36	36	36	38	40	42	42	44	46	48	50	52	52	54	58	58	60	64	64	64
	330	28	28	30	30	32	32	34	34	34	36	36	38	40	42	44	44	46	48	50	50	52	54	58	58	60	64	64	64
	331	28	28	30	30	32	32	34	34	34	36	36	38	40	42	44	44	46	48	50	52	52	54	58	58	60	64	64	64
	332	28	28	30	30	32	32	34	34	34	36	36	38	40	42	42	44	46	48	50	52	52	54	58	58	60	64	64	66
	333	28	28	30	30	32	32	34	34	34	36	36	38	40	42	42	44	46	48	50	50	52	54	56	58	60	62	64	66
	334	28	28	30	30	32	32	34	34	34	36	36	38	40	42	42	44	46	48	50	50	52	54	54	58	60	62	64	66
	335	28	28	30	30	32	32	34	34	34	36	36	38	40	42	42	44	46	48	50	50	52	54	56	58	60	62	64	66
	336	28	28	30	30	32	32	34	34	34	36	36	38	40	42	42	44	46	48	50	50	52	54	56	58	60	62	64	66
	337	28	28	30	30	32	32	34	34	34	36	36	38	40	42	42	44	46	48	48	50	52	54	56	58	60	62	64	66
	338	28	28	30	30	32	32	34	34	34	36	36	38	40	42	42	44	46	46	50	50	52	54	56	58	60	62	64	66
	339	28	28	30	30	32	32	32	34	34	36	36	38	40	42	42	44	46	46	50	50	52	54	56	58	60	62	64	66
	340	28	28	30	30	32	32	32	34	34	36	36	38	40	40	42	44	46	46	48	50	52	54	56	58	60	62	64	66
	341	28	28	30	30	32	32	32	34	34	36	36	38	40	40	42	44	46	46	48	50	52	54	56	58	60	62	64	66
	342	28	28	30	30	32	32	32	34	34	36	36	38	40	40	42	44	46	48	48	50	52	54	56	58	60	62	64	66
	343	28	28	30	30	32	32	32	34	34	36	36	38	40	40	42	44	46	46	48	50	52	54	56	58	60	62	64	66
	344	28	28	30	30	30	32	32	34	34	36	36	38	40	40	42	44	46	46	48	50	52	54	56	58	60	62	64	66
	345	28	28	30	30	30	32	32	34	34	36	36	38	40	40	42	44	46	46	48	50	52	54	56	58	60	62	64	66
	346	28	28	30	30	30	32	32	34	34	34	36	36	38	40	42	44	46	46	48	50	52	54	56	58	60	62	64	66
	347	28	28	30	30	30	32	32	34	34	36	36	36	40	40	42	44	46	46	48	50	52	54	56	58	60	62	64	66
	348	28	28	28	30	30	32	32	34	34	34	36	36	40	40	42	44	46	46	48	50	52	54	56	58	60	62	64	66
	349	28	28	28	30	30	32	32	34	34	36	36	36	40	40	42	44	46	46	48	50	52	54	56	58	60	62	64	66
	350	26	28	28	30	30	32	32	34	34	34	36	36	40	40	42	44	46	46	48	50	52	52	56	58	60	62	64	66

CONTINUED...

Geographical and Chronological Social Security Numbers

YEAR

STATE OR POSSESSION	AREA	51	52	53	54	55	56	57	58	59	60	61	62	63	64	65	66	67	68	69	70	71	72	73	74	75	76	77	78
ILLINOIS	351	26	28	28	30	30	32	32	34	34	34	36	36	40	40	42	44	46	46	48	50	52	52	56	58	60	62	64	64
	352	28	28	28	30	30	32	32	34	34	34	36	36	38	40	42	44	44	46	48	50	52	52	56	58	60	62	64	64
	353	26	28	28	30	30	32	32	34	34	34	36	36	40	40	42	44	44	46	48	50	52	52	56	58	60	62	64	64
	354	26	28	28	30	30	32	32	34	34	34	36	36	40	40	42	44	44	46	48	50	52	52	56	58	60	62	64	64
	355	28	28	28	30	30	32	32	34	34	34	36	36	40	40	42	44	46	46	48	50	52	52	56	58	60	62	64	66
	356	26	28	28	30	30	32	32	32	34	34	36	36	40	40	42	44	44	46	48	50	52	52	56	58	60	62	64	64
	357	28	28	28	30	30	32	32	32	34	34	36	36	40	40	42	44	44	46	48	50	52	52	56	58	60	62	64	64
	358	26	28	28	30	30	32	32	34	34	34	36	36	38	40	42	44	44	46	48	50	52	52	56	58	60	62	64	64
	359	26	28	28	30	30	32	32	32	34	34	36	36	40	40	42	44	46	46	48	50	52	52	56	58	60	62	64	64
	360	26	28	28	30	30	32	32	32	34	34	36	36	38	40	42	44	44	46	48	50	52	52	56	58	60	62	64	64
	361	26	28	28	30	30	32	32	32	34	34	36	36	38	40	42	44	44	46	48	50	52	52	56	58	60	62	64	64
MICHIGAN	362	34	36	36	38	38	40	42	42	44	44	44	46	48	50	54	56	56	60	62	62	64	66	72	74	76	80	82	84
	363	34	36	36	38	38	40	42	42	42	44	44	46	48	50	52	54	58	58	60	64	66	66	72	74	76	80	82	84
	364	34	36	36	38	38	40	42	42	42	44	44	46	48	50	52	54	56	60	60	62	64	66	72	74	76	80	82	84
	365	34	34	36	36	38	40	40	42	42	44	44	46	50	50	52	54	56	60	60	62	64	66	72	74	76	80	82	84
	366	34	34	36	38	38	40	42	42	42	44	44	46	48	50	52	54	56	58	60	62	64	66	70	74	76	80	82	84
	367	34	34	36	36	38	40	40	42	42	44	44	46	48	50	52	54	56	58	60	62	64	66	70	74	76	80	82	84
	368	34	34	36	36	38	40	40	42	42	44	44	46	48	50	52	54	56	58	60	62	64	66	70	74	76	80	82	84
	369	34	34	36	36	38	40	40	42	42	44	44	46	48	50	52	54	56	58	60	62	64	66	70	74	76	80	82	84
	370	34	34	36	36	38	40	40	42	42	44	44	46	48	50	52	54	56	58	60	62	64	66	70	72	74	78	82	84
	371	34	34	36	36	38	40	40	40	47	44	44	46	48	50	52	54	54	58	60	62	64	66	70	72	74	78	82	84
	372	32	34	36	36	38	40	40	42	42	44	44	46	48	50	52	54	56	58	60	62	64	66	70	72	74	78	82	84
	373	32	34	36	36	38	40	40	42	42	44	44	46	48	50	52	54	56	58	60	62	64	66	70	72	74	78	82	82
	374	34	34	36	36	38	40	40	40	47	44	44	46	48	50	52	54	56	58	60	62	64	66	70	72	74	78	82	82
	375	34	34	36	36	38	40	40	40	47	44	44	46	48	50	52	54	56	58	60	62	64	66	70	72	74	78	82	82

CONTINUED...

Geographical and Chronological Social Security Numbers

YEAR

STATE OR POSSESSION	AREA	51	52	53	54	55	56	57	58	59	60	61	62	63	64	65	66	67	68	69	70	71	72	73	74	75	76	77	78
MICHIGAN	376	32	34	36	36	38	40	40	40	42	44	44	46	48	50	52	54	56	58	60	62	64	66	70	72	74	78	82	78
	377	32	34	36	36	38	38	40	40	42	42	44	46	48	50	52	54	56	58	60	62	64	66	70	72	74	78	82	82
	378	32	34	36	36	38	38	40	40	42	42	44	46	48	50	52	54	56	58	60	62	64	66	70	72	74	78	80	82
	379	32	34	36	36	38	38	40	40	42	42	44	44	48	50	52	54	56	58	60	62	64	64	70	72	74	78	80	82
	380	32	34	34	36	38	38	40	40	42	42	44	44	48	50	52	54	56	58	60	62	64	64	70	72	74	78	80	82
	381	32	34	34	36	38	38	40	40	42	42	44	44	48	50	52	54	56	58	60	62	64	64	70	72	74	78	80	80
	382	32	34	34	36	38	38	40	40	42	42	44	44	48	50	52	54	56	58	60	62	64	64	70	72	74	78	80	80
	383	32	34	34	36	38	38	40	40	42	42	44	44	48	50	52	54	56	58	60	62	64	64	70	72	74	78	80	80
	384	32	34	34	36	36	38	40	40	42	42	44	44	48	50	50	54	54	58	60	60	64	64	70	72	74	78	80	80
	385	32	34	34	36	36	38	40	40	40	42	44	44	48	48	52	54	54	58	60	60	62	64	70	72	74	78	80	80
	386	32	34	34	36	38	38	40	40	40	42	44	44	48	48	52	54	54	58	60	60	64	64	70	72	74	78	80	80
WISCONSIN	387	32	34	34	36	36	38	40	40	42	42	44	44	48	50	52	54	56	58	60	62	64	66	70	74	76	80	82	80
	388	32	32	34	34	36	38	40	40	42	42	44	44	48	50	52	54	56	58	60	62	64	66	70	74	76	80	82	80
	389	32	32	34	34	36	38	40	40	42	42	44	44	48	50	52	54	56	58	60	62	64	66	70	74	76	80	82	80
	390	32	32	34	34	36	38	40	40	40	42	44	44	48	50	52	54	56	58	60	62	64	66	70	72	76	78	80	80
	391	32	32	34	34	36	38	40	40	40	42	44	44	48	50	52	54	56	58	60	62	64	66	70	72	76	78	80	80
	392	32	32	34	34	36	38	40	40	40	42	44	44	48	50	52	54	56	58	60	62	64	66	70	72	76	78	80	80
	393	30	32	32	34	36	38	38	40	40	42	44	44	48	50	52	54	56	58	60	62	64	66	70	72	74	78	80	80
	394	32	32	32	34	36	38	38	38	40	42	44	44	48	50	52	54	56	58	60	62	64	64	70	72	74	78	80	80
	395	30	32	32	34	36	38	38	38	40	42	44	44	46	48	50	54	56	58	58	60	62	64	70	72	74	78	80	80
	396	30	32	32	34	36	38	38	38	40	42	44	44	48	48	50	54	56	58	58	60	64	64	70	72	74	78	80	80
	397	30	32	32	34	36	38	38	38	40	42	44	44	48	48	50	54	56	58	60	60	62	64	70	72	74	78	80	80
	398	30	32	32	34	34	36	38	38	40	40	44	44	48	48	50	54	54	56	58	60	62	64	70	72	74	78	80	80
	399	30	32	32	34	34	36	38	38	40	40	44	44	48	48	50	54	54	58	60	60	66	64	70	72	74	78	80	80
KENTUCKY	400	44	46	48	50	52	54	56	56	58	60	60	62	66	68	72	74	76	78	82	84	86	88	94	98	04	06	08	11

CONTINUED...

Geographical and Chronological Social Security Numbers

STATE OR POSSESSION	AREA	51	52	53	54	55	56	57	58	59	60	61	62	63	64	65	66	67	68	69	70	71	72	73	74	75	76	77	78
KENTUCKY	401	44	46	48	48	52	54	56	56	58	58	60	62	66	68	70	74	76	78	80	84	86	88	94	98	04	06	08	11
	402	44	46	48	48	50	54	54	56	58	58	60	62	66	68	70	74	76	78	80	84	86	88	92	96	04	06	08	11
	403	42	46	46	48	50	54	54	56	56	58	60	62	66	66	70	72	76	78	80	82	86	88	92	96	02	06	08	11
	404	44	44	46	48	50	52	54	56	56	58	60	62	64	64	70	72	74	78	80	82	86	88	92	96	02	06	08	11
	405	44	44	46	48	50	52	54	54	56	58	60	62	64	66	70	72	76	78	80	82	86	88	92	96	02	06	08	11
	406	42	44	46	48	50	52	54	56	56	58	60	62	64	66	70	72	74	76	80	82	84	88	92	96	02	06	08	11
TENNESSEE	407	42	44	46	48	50	52	54	54	56	58	58	60	64	66	68	72	74	76	78	82	84	86	92	96	02	04	08	08
	408	54	56	58	58	62	64	66	66	68	70	72	74	78	80	84	86	90	92	96	98	02	06	15	19	23	27	29	29
	409	54	54	56	58	62	64	66	66	68	70	72	74	78	80	84	88	90	92	94	98	04	06	15	19	23	22	27	29
	410	54	54	56	58	62	64	66	66	68	70	72	74	78	80	84	88	90	92	94	98	02	04	13	19	23	25	27	29
	411	52	54	56	58	60	62	64	66	68	70	72	74	78	80	84	88	90	92	94	98	02	04	13	19	21	25	27	29
	412	52	54	56	58	60	62	64	66	68	70	72	74	78	80	84	86	88	92	94	98	02	04	13	17	21	25	27	29
	413	52	54	56	58	60	62	64	66	68	70	72	74	76	80	82	86	88	92	94	96	02	04	13	17	21	25	27	29
	414	52	54	56	58	60	62	64	66	68	70	72	72	76	80	84	86	88	92	94	96	02	04	13	17	21	25	27	29
	415	52	54	56	58	60	62	64	66	68	68	70	72	76	78	92	96	88	90	94	96	02	04	13	17	21	25	27	29
ALABAMA	416	44	46	46	48	50	52	54	54	56	58	60	62	64	66	70	72	74	76	78	80	82	84	90	94	96	02	04	06
	417	44	44	46	48	50	52	54	54	56	58	60	60	64	66	70	72	74	76	78	80	82	84	90	94	96	02	04	04
	418	42	44	46	48	50	52	54	54	56	58	60	60	64	66	68	72	76	76	78	80	82	84	90	94	96	98	02	04
	419	44	44	46	48	50	52	52	54	56	58	58	60	64	66	70	72	74	74	78	80	82	84	90	94	96	98	02	04
	420	44	44	46	48	50	52	52	54	56	58	58	60	64	66	68	70	72	76	78	80	82	84	90	92	96	98	02	04
	421	42	44	46	48	50	50	52	54	56	58	58	60	64	64	68	70	74	74	76	78	80	82	90	92	96	98	02	04
	422	44	44	46	46	48	50	52	54	56	56	58	60	62	64	68	72	74	74	76	78	80	82	88	92	96	98	02	04
	423	42	44	44	46	48	50	52	54	54	56	58	60	62	64	68	70	72	74	76	78	80	84	88	92	94	98	02	04
	424	42	44	44	46	48	50	52	54	54	56	58	60	62	64	68	70	72	74	76	78	80	82	88	92	94	98	02	04
MISSISSIPPI	425	62	64	68	70	74	78	82	84	86	88	90	94	98	98	98	98	98	98	98	02	08	11	17	21	25	29	31	33

YEAR

CONTINUED...

Geographical and Chronological Social Security Numbers

YEAR

STATE OR POSSESSION	AREA	51	52	53	54	55	56	57	58	59	60	61	62	63	64	65	66	67	68	69	70	71	72	73	74	75	76	77	78
MISSISSIPPI	426	60	64	68	70	74	78	80	82	86	88	90	92	98	98	98	98	98	98	98	02	06	11	17	21	25	29	31	33
	427	60	64	66	68	74	78	80	82	84	88	90	92	96	98	98	98	98	98	98	02	06	11	15	21	25	29	29	31
	428	62	64	66	68	74	76	80	80	84	86	90	92	96	98	98	98	98	98	98	02	06	11	15	19	23	29	29	31
ARKANSAS	429	62	62	66	66	70	74	74	76	78	80	82	86	88	90	96	98	02	04	08	11	15	17	25	29	33	35	39	41
	430	60	62	64	66	70	72	74	75	78	80	82	84	88	90	96	98	02	04	06	11	13	17	23	27	31	35	37	39
	431	60	62	64	66	70	72	74	75	78	80	82	84	88	90	94	98	02	04	06	11	13	17	23	27	31	35	37	39
	432	60	62	64	66	68	72	74	75	76	78	82	84	88	90	94	98	02	04	06	11	13	15	23	27	31	34	37	39
LOUISIANA	433	48	50	52	54	56	58	60	60	62	64	66	68	72	74	80	84	86	90	94	98	02	06	15	19	25	29	33	35
	434	48	50	52	52	54	56	58	60	62	64	64	68	72	74	78	82	86	90	92	98	02	06	15	19	25	29	33	35
	435	48	50	52	52	54	56	58	60	62	64	66	66	72	74	78	82	86	88	92	96	02	06	13	19	25	29	31	35
	436	48	50	52	52	54	56	58	60	62	62	64	66	72	74	76	82	86	88	92	96	02	06	13	19	23	29	31	35
	437	48	48	50	52	54	56	58	60	60	62	64	66	72	74	78	82	84	88	92	96	02	06	13	19	23	29	31	35
	438	46	48	50	52	54	56	58	60	60	62	64	68	70	74	78	82	86	88	92	96	02	06	13	19	23	27	31	33
	439	48	48	50	52	54	56	58	58	60	62	64	66	70	74	78	82	84	88	92	96	02	04	13	17	23	27	31	33
OKLAHOMA	440	34	36	36	38	38	40	42	42	44	44	46	46	48	50	52	54	54	56	58	60	62	62	66	68	70	72	74	74
	441	34	34	36	36	38	40	40	42	42	44	44	46	48	50	52	54	54	56	58	60	62	62	66	68	70	72	74	74
	442	32	34	36	36	38	40	40	42	42	44	44	46	48	50	52	54	54	56	58	60	60	62	66	68	70	72	74	74
	443	34	34	36	36	38	40	40	42	42	44	44	46	48	50	52	54	54	56	58	60	60	62	66	68	70	72	74	76
	444	32	34	34	36	38	40	40	42	42	44	44	46	48	48	50	52	54	56	56	58	60	62	64	66	68	70	72	74
	445	34	34	34	36	38	40	40	40	42	42	44	46	48	48	50	52	54	56	56	58	60	62	66	68	70	72	72	74
	446	34	34	34	36	38	40	40	40	42	42	44	46	46	48	50	52	54	54	56	58	60	62	64	66	70	72	72	74
	447	32	34	34	36	38	40	40	40	42	42	44	44	46	48	50	52	54	54	56	58	60	62	66	66	70	72	72	74
	448	32	34	34	36	38	40	40	40	42	42	44	44	46	48	50	52	52	54	56	58	58	60	64	66	70	72	72	74
TEXAS	449	54	56	58	58	62	64	66	68	70	72	74	76	80	84	88	92	96	98	06	08	13	15	25	29	35	39	41	45
	450	52	56	58	58	62	64	66	68	70	72	74	76	80	84	88	92	94	98	04	06	13	15	23	29	35	39	41	45

CONTINUED...

Geographical and Chronological Social Security Numbers

STATE OR POSSESSION	AREA	YEAR																											
		51	52	53	54	55	56	57	58	59	60	61	62	63	64	65	66	67	68	69	70	71	72	73	74	75	76	77	78
TEXAS	451	54	56	58	58	62	64	66	68	70	72	74	76	82	84	88	92	96	98	04	08	13	15	23	29	33	39	41	45
	452	52	56	58	58	62	64	66	68	70	72	74	76	80	84	88	92	96	98	04	08	11	15	23	29	33	39	41	45
	453	54	54	56	58	62	64	66	68	70	72	74	76	80	84	88	92	94	98	04	08	13	15	23	29	33	39	41	43
	454	52	56	56	58	62	64	66	68	70	72	72	76	80	82	88	92	94	98	04	06	13	15	23	29	33	39	41	43
	455	54	54	56	58	60	64	66	68	70	72	72	76	80	84	88	92	94	98	04	08	13	15	23	29	33	39	41	43
	456	54	54	56	58	60	64	66	66	68	70	74	76	80	84	88	92	94	98	04	06	13	15	23	29	33	37	41	43
	457	52	54	56	58	60	64	66	68	70	72	72	76	80	82	88	90	94	98	04	08	11	15	23	29	33	37	41	43
	458	52	54	58	58	60	64	66	68	70	72	72	76	80	82	88	92	94	98	04	06	11	13	23	29	33	37	41	43
	459	52	54	56	58	60	64	66	68	70	72	72	76	80	82	86	90	94	98	02	06	11	13	23	29	33	37	39	43
	460	52	54	56	58	60	64	66	66	68	70	72	74	80	82	86	92	94	98	04	06	11	13	23	27	33	37	41	43
	461	52	54	56	58	60	62	66	66	68	70	72	74	80	82	86	90	94	96	02	06	11	13	23	27	33	37	39	43
	462	52	54	56	58	60	64	66	66	68	70	72	76	80	82	86	90	94	98	02	06	11	13	23	27	33	37	39	43
	463	52	54	56	58	60	62	64	66	68	70	72	74	30	82	86	90	94	96	02	06	11	13	23	27	33	37	39	43
	464	52	54	56	58	60	64	64	66	68	70	72	76	80	82	88	90	94	98	02	06	11	13	23	29	33	37	37	43
	465	52	54	56	58	60	64	64	66	68	70	72	74	80	82	86	90	94	96	02	06	11	13	23	27	33	37	39	43
	466	52	54	56	58	60	62	64	66	68	70	72	74	80	82	86	90	92	98	02	06	8	13	23	27	33	37	39	43
	467	52	54	56	56	60	62	64	66	68	70	72	74	78	82	84	90	94	96	02	06	11	13	23	27	33	37	39	43
MINNESOTA	468	36	38	38	40	42	44	46	46	48	48	50	52	56	56	58	62	64	66	68	70	72	74	80	82	84	84	90	90
	469	36	36	38	40	42	44	46	48	48	48	50	52	56	56	58	60	64	66	68	70	72	74	78	82	84	84	90	90
	470	34	36	38	40	42	44	44	46	48	48	50	52	54	56	58	62	64	64	68	70	72	74	78	80	84	84	90	90
	471	36	36	38	38	42	44	44	46	46	48	50	50	54	56	58	60	62	64	66	68	70	72	78	82	84	88	88	90
	472	34	36	38	38	42	44	44	46	46	48	50	52	54	56	58	60	62	64	66	68	70	72	78	82	84	88	88	90
	473	34	36	38	38	40	44	44	46	46	48	50	50	54	56	58	60	62	64	66	68	70	72	78	80	84	88	88	90
	474	36	36	38	38	40	42	44	44	46	48	48	50	54	54	58	60	62	64	66	68	70	72	78	80	84	88	88	90
	475	34	36	36	38	40	42	44	44	46	48	48	50	54	56	58	60	62	64	66	68	70	72	78	80	84	88	88	90

CONTINUED...

Geographical and Chronological Social Security Numbers

YEAR

STATE OR POSSESSION	AREA	51	52	53	54	55	56	57	58	59	60	61	62	63	64	65	66	67	68	69	70	71	72	73	74	75	76	77	78
MINNESOTA	476	34	36	36	38	40	42	44	44	46	48	48	50	54	56	58	60	62	64	66	68	70	72	78	80	84	84	88	90
	477	34	36	36	38	40	42	44	44	46	46	48	50	52	56	56	60	62	64	66	68	70	72	78	80	82	82	88	90
IOWA	478	36	38	40	42	46	48	50	50	52	52	54	56	62	62	66	68	70	72	74	76	78	78	84	86	88	88	94	94
	479	36	38	40	42	44	48	48	50	52	52	54	56	58	62	66	68	70	72	74	74	78	78	84	86	88	88	94	94
	480	38	38	40	40	44	48	48	50	50	52	54	56	60	62	64	66	68	70	72	74	76	78	82	86	88	88	94	94
	481	38	38	40	40	44	48	48	50	52	54	54	54	58	62	64	66	68	72	72	74	76	78	82	86	88	88	92	94
	482	38	38	40	40	44	48	48	50	50	52	54	54	58	62	64	66	68	70	72	74	76	78	82	86	88	88	92	94
	483	36	38	40	40	44	48	48	48	50	52	52	54	56	62	64	66	68	70	72	74	76	78	82	86	88	88	92	94
	484	36	38	38	40	44	46	48	48	50	52	52	54	58	62	64	66	68	70	72	74	76	78	82	84	88	88	92	94
	485	34	38	38	40	42	46	48	48	50	52	52	54	58	60	64	66	68	70	72	74	76	78	82	84	88	88	92	94
MISSOURI	486	38	38	40	40	42	44	44	46	46	48	48	50	52	54	56	56	58	60	62	64	66	66	70	72	74	74	80	80
	487	38	38	40	40	42	44	44	46	46	48	48	50	52	54	54	58	58	60	62	64	66	66	70	72	74	74	80	80
	488	36	38	40	40	42	44	44	46	46	48	48	50	52	52	56	56	58	60	62	64	66	66	70	72	74	74	80	80
	489	36	38	40	40	42	44	44	44	46	46	48	50	52	52	56	56	58	60	62	64	66	66	70	72	74	74	80	80
	490	36	38	38	40	42	44	44	44	46	46	48	50	52	52	54	56	58	60	62	64	64	66	70	72	74	74	78	80
	491	36	38	38	40	42	42	44	44	46	46	48	48	52	52	54	54	58	60	62	62	64	66	70	72	74	74	78	80
	492	36	38	38	40	42	44	44	44	46	46	48	48	52	52	54	56	58	60	62	62	64	66	70	72	74	74	78	80
	493	36	38	38	40	42	42	44	44	46	46	48	48	50	52	54	54	58	60	62	62	64	66	70	72	74	74	78	80
	494	36	38	38	40	42	42	44	44	46	46	48	48	52	52	54	56	58	60	60	62	64	66	70	72	74	74	78	80
	495	36	38	38	40	42	42	44	44	46	46	48	48	50	52	54	56	58	58	60	62	64	66	68	72	74	74	78	80
	496	36	36	38	38	40	42	44	44	44	46	48	48	50	52	54	56	58	58	60	62	64	66	68	72	74	74	78	80
	497	36	36	38	38	40	42	44	44	44	46	46	48	50	52	54	56	56	58	60	62	64	66	68	70	74	74	78	80
	498	36	36	38	38	40	42	42	44	44	46	46	48	50	52	54	56	56	58	60	62	64	66	68	70	72	74	78	80
	499	36	36	38	38	40	42	42	44	44	46	46	48	50	52	54	56	56	58	60	62	64	66	68	70	74	72	78	80
	500	36	36	38	38	40	42	42	44	44	46	46	48	50	52	54	56	56	68	60	62	64	66	68	70	72	72	78	78

CONTINUED...

Geographical and Chronological Social Security Numbers

YEAR

STATE OR POSSESSION	AREA	51	52	53	54	55	56	57	58	59	60	61	62	63	64	65	66	67	68	69	70	71	72	73	74	75	76	77	78
N. DAKOTA	501	30	32	34	34	40	42	44	44	46	48	48	50	54	54	56	60	60	64	68	70	74	78	84	88	90	90	92	78
	502	32	32	32	34	36	40	42	44	44	46	48	50	52	54	56	58	60	62	64	70	72	76	84	86	82	88	92	92
S. DAKOTA	503	34	34	36	38	42	46	46	48	48	50	52	54	58	60	60	64	66	68	70	72	76	78	84	86	90	90	92	92
	504	32	34	36	36	40	44	46	46	48	50	50	54	56	58	60	62	64	66	68	72	74	76	84	86	90	90	92	94
NEBRASKA	505	40	42	42	44	48	52	52	54	54	56	58	60	62	64	66	70	72	74	76	78	82	84	88	92	94	94	98	92
	506	38	40	42	44	46	50	52	52	54	56	56	58	64	64	66	70	72	74	76	78	80	84	88	92	94	94	98	02
	507	40	40	42	42	46	50	52	52	54	54	56	58	62	64	66	68	70	74	76	78	80	82	88	90	94	94	98	02
	508	38	40	40	42	46	50	50	52	54	54	56	58	62	64	66	68	70	74	76	78	80	82	88	90	94	94	96	98
KANSAS	509	32	34	36	36	38	40	42	42	44	44	46	46	52	52	54	56	56	58	60	62	64	66	72	74	76	78	78	80
	510	32	34	34	36	38	40	42	42	44	44	46	46	50	52	54	54	56	58	60	62	64	66	70	74	76	78	78	80
	511	32	34	34	36	38	40	40	42	42	44	46	46	50	52	52	54	56	58	60	62	64	66	70	72	74	76	78	78
	512	32	32	34	36	38	40	40	42	42	44	44	46	50	50	52	54	56	58	60	62	64	66	70	72	74	76	78	78
	513	30	32	34	34	38	40	40	42	42	44	44	46	48	50	52	54	56	58	60	62	64	64	70	72	74	76	78	78
	514	32	32	34	34	36	40	40	40	42	42	44	46	50	50	52	54	56	58	60	62	64	64	70	72	74	76	78	78
	515	32	32	34	34	36	38	40	40	42	42	44	46	48	50	52	54	56	56	58	60	62	64	70	72	74	76	76	78
MONTANA	516	36	38	40	40	42	46	46	48	48	50	52	54	56	58	60	64	66	66	70	72	74	76	86	88	90	94	94	94
	517	36	38	38	40	42	44	46	46	48	50	50	52	56	58	60	62	64	66	68	70	72	74	84	88	90	92	92	92
IDAHO	518	38	38	40	40	42	44	46	48	48	50	52	54	58	58	60	64	66	68	70	72	74	76	86	88	92	94	94	94
	519	36	36	38	40	42	44	44	46	46	48	50	52	56	56	58	60	62	64	66	68	70	72	84	88	90	92	94	94
WYOMING	520	36	36	38	40	42	44	44	46	46	48	50	52	56	56	58	60	62	64	66	68	70	72	80	84	86	88	90	90
COLORADO	521	42	44	46	48	50	52	52	54	56	58	60	62	66	68	72	74	78	80	84	88	90	94	02	08	13	17	21	21
	522	42	44	46	46	52	50	52	54	54	56	58	60	66	68	72	74	78	80	84	86	90	94	02	06	13	17	21	23
	523	42	42	44	46	50	50	52	52	54	56	58	60	##	68	70	74	76	80	82	86	90	94	02	06	11	17	19	23
	524	42	42	44	46	48	50	52	52	54	56	58	60	64	66	72	74	76	80	84	86	90	94	98	06	11	15	19	21
NEW MEXICO	525	74	76	80	84	86	92	96	98	98	98	98	98	98	98	98	98	98	98	98	98	98	98	08	15	19	23	25	27

CONTINUED....

Geographical and Chronological Social Security Numbers

STATE OR POSSESSION	AREA	51	52	53	54	55	56	57	58	59	60	61	62	63	64	65	66	67	68	69	70	71	72	73	74	75	76	77	78
ARIZONA	526	44	44	46	48	52	54	56	60	62	64	68	72	78	80	86	90	96	02	08	17	21	27	41	51	59	65	71	75
	527	42	44	46	48	50	54	56	58	60	64	66	70	74	82	84	92	96	02	08	15	21	29	41	49	57	65	69	75
UTAH	528	44	44	46	48	50	52	54	56	58	60	62	64	68	70	72	76	80	86	88	90	92	94	06	13	17	21	23	25
	529	42	44	46	48	50	52	52	54	56	58	60	64	68	70	72	74	80	84	86	88	92	94	06	11	15	19	21	25
NEVADA	530	20	22	22	24	24	26	26	28	28	30	30	32	36	36	38	42	44	46	50	52	56	58	70	74	78	82	84	84
WASHINGTON	531	32	34	34	34	38	38	40	40	40	42	44	44	48	50	52	54	56	58	60	62	64	64	70	72	74	78	80	82
	532	32	34	36	34	36	38	38	40	40	42	42	44	48	50	52	54	56	58	60	62	64	64	70	72	74	78	80	82
	533	32	32	34	34	36	38	38	40	40	42	42	44	48	48	50	54	56	58	60	60	64	64	68	72	74	78	80	82
	534	32	32	34	34	36	38	38	40	40	42	42	44	48	48	50	54	56	56	58	60	64	64	68	70	74	78	80	82
	535	32	32	32	34	36	38	38	38	40	40	42	44	46	48	50	52	54	56	60	60	62	64	68	70	74	76	80	82
	536	32	32	32	34	36	36	38	38	40	40	42	44	46	48	50	52	54	56	58	60	62	64	68	70	74	76	80	82
	537	30	32	32	34	36	36	38	38	40	42	42	44	46	48	50	52	54	56	58	60	62	64	68	70	74	76	78	80
	538	30	30	32	34	36	36	38	38	40	40	42	44	46	48	50	52	54	56	58	60	62	64	68	70	72	76	78	80
	539	30	32	32	34	36	36	38	38	40	40	42	42	46	48	50	52	54	56	58	60	62	64	68	70	72	76	78	80
OREGON	540	36	38	40	40	44	46	46	48	48	50	50	52	56	58	60	62	64	66	68	70	74	76	80	84	88	90	92	94
	541	36	38	40	40	44	44	46	46	48	48	50	52	56	58	60	62	64	66	68	72	74	76	80	84	88	90	92	94
	542	36	38	38	40	42	44	46	48	48	48	50	52	56	56	60	62	64	66	68	72	74	74	80	84	86	90	92	94
	543	36	36	38	38	42	44	44	46	46	48	50	52	54	56	58	60	64	64	68	72	74	74	80	84	86	90	92	94
	544	36	36	38	40	42	44	44	46	46	48	50	50	54	56	58	60	64	64	66	72	74	80	82	86	90	90	90	92
CALIFORNIA	545	46	48	50	50	52	54	56	58	60	62	64	68	72	76	80	86	88	92	98	04	11	19	27	33	39	45	49	53
	546	44	48	48	50	52	54	56	58	60	62	64	68	74	76	80	84	88	92	96	04	11	19	27	33	39	45	49	53
	547	46	48	50	50	52	54	56	58	60	62	64	68	72	76	80	86	88	92	98	04	11	19	29	33	39	45	49	53
	548	46	46	48	50	52	54	56	58	60	62	64	66	72	76	80	84	88	92	96	04	11	19	27	33	39	45	49	53
	549	46	46	48	50	52	54	56	58	60	62	64	68	72	76	80	84	88	92	96	02	08	19	27	33	39	45	49	53
	550	46	46	48	50	52	54	56	58	60	62	64	68	72	76	80	84	88	92	96	04	11	19	27	33	39	45	49	53

YEAR

Geographical and Chronological Social Security Numbers

YEAR

STATE OR POSSESSION	AREA	51	52	53	54	55	56	57	58	59	60	61	62	63	64	65	66	67	68	69	70	71	72	73	74	75	76	77	78
CALIFORNIA	551	46	46	48	50	52	54	56	58	60	62	64	68	72	76	78	84	88	92	96	02	11	17	27	33	39	45	49	53
	552	46	46	48	50	52	54	56	58	60	62	64	66	72	76	78	86	88	92	96	02	08	19	27	33	39	45	49	53
	553	46	46	48	50	52	54	56	58	60	60	64	66	72	76	80	82	88	92	96	02	11	19	27	33	39	43	49	53
	554	44	46	48	50	52	54	56	58	58	62	64	66	72	76	80	84	88	92	96	04	11	19	27	33	39	43	49	53
	555	44	46	48	50	52	54	56	56	58	62	64	66	72	74	80	84	88	92	96	04	11	17	27	33	37	43	49	53
	556	44	46	48	50	52	54	56	56	58	62	64	66	72	74	80	84	88	92	96	04	11	17	27	33	37	43	49	53
	557	44	46	48	50	52	54	56	56	58	62	64	66	72	74	80	82	88	92	96	02	11	19	27	33	37	43	49	50
	558	44	46	48	50	52	54	56	56	58	60	62	66	72	74	80	84	88	92	96	02	11	19	27	33	37	43	49	53
	559	44	46	48	50	52	54	56	56	58	60	64	68	70	74	80	84	86	92	96	04	08	19	27	33	37	43	49	53
	560	44	46	48	50	52	54	56	56	58	60	64	66	72	74	80	84	88	90	96	04	08	19	27	33	37	43	49	53
	561	46	46	48	50	52	54	56	56	58	60	62	66	70	74	78	82	86	92	96	02	11	19	23	27	33	43	49	53
	562	44	46	48	50	52	54	56	56	58	60	62	66	70	74	78	82	86	92	94	02	08	17	27	33	37	43	49	53
	563	44	46	48	50	52	54	56	56	58	60	62	66	72	74	80	82	86	92	96	02	08	17	27	33	37	43	49	53
	564	44	46	48	50	52	54	56	56	58	60	62	66	70	74	78	82	86	90	96	02	08	17	27	33	37	43	49	53
	565	44	46	48	50	52	54	56	56	58	60	62	66	72	74	78	86	86	92	96	02	08	17	27	33	37	43	49	53
	566	44	46	48	48	50	52	54	56	58	60	62	66	72	74	80	82	88	92	96	02	08	17	27	33	37	43	49	53
	567	44	46	48	48	50	52	54	56	58	60	62	66	72	74	78	82	86	92	96	02	08	17	27	31	37	43	49	53
	568	44	46	48	48	50	52	54	56	58	60	62	66	70	74	78	82	86	92	96	02	08	17	27	31	37	43	49	53
	569	44	46	46	48	50	52	54	56	58	60	62	66	72	74	78	82	86	92	96	02	08	17	27	31	37	43	49	53
	570	44	46	48	48	50	52	54	56	58	60	62	66	70	74	78	82	88	90	96	98	08	17	27	31	37	43	47	59
	571	44	46	46	48	50	52	54	56	58	60	62	66	72	74	78	82	86	90	96	02	08	17	27	31	37	43	47	53
	572	44	46	46	48	50	52	54	56	58	60	62	66	70	74	78	82	86	90	96	02	08	17	25	31	37	43	47	53
	573	44	46	46	48	50	52	54	56	58	60	62	66	70	74	78	82	86	90	94	02	08	17	27	31	37	43	47	53
ALASKA	574	10	10	12	12	12	12	14	14	14	14	16	18	18	18	20	22	24	24	26	28	30	32	32	54	56	58	58	60
HAWAII	575	32	36	36	36	36	38	40	40	42	44	46	48	50	52	56	58	62	64	68	72	76	78	88	92	96	04	06	06

CONTINUED...

Geographical and Chronological Social Security Numbers

YEAR

STATE OR POSSESSION	AREA	51	52	53	54	55	56	57	58	59	60	61	62	63	64	65	66	67	68	69	70	71	72	73	74	75	76	77	78
HAWAII	576	30	32	32	36	36	38	38	40	42	44	44	48	50	52	56	58	60	64	66	72	74	76	88	92	96	02	04	04
DISTRICT OF	577	46	48	50	52	52	52	54	56	56	58	60	60	64	64	66	68	72	74	74	76	78	80	86	88	92	96	96	98
COLUMBIA	578	48	46	48	50	52	52	54	54	56	56	58	60	62	64	66	68	70	74	74	76	78	80	86	88	92	94	96	96
	579	30	48	48	48	50	52	54	54	54	56	58	60	62	64	66	68	70	72	74	76	78	80	84	88	90	94	96	96
U.S. VIRGIN ISLANDS	580	28	40	48	54	62	66	72	78	82	86	92	96	98	98	98	98	98	98	98	98	98	16	02	04	06	06	08	08
PUERTO RICO	581	28	40	48	52	60	68	74	78	80	86	92	96	98	98	98	98	98	98	98	98	98	98	11	19	23	41	55	63
	582	-	40	48	52	60	66	72	76	80	86	92	96	98	98	98	98	98	98	98	98	98	98	11	17	23	41	55	61
	583	-	-	-	-	-	-	-	-	-	-	-	-	07	10	22	34	46	54	64	74	84	94	11	17	23	39	55	61
	584	-	-	-	-	-	-	-	-	-	-	-	-	03	10	18	34	40	50	62	74	84	92	08	17	23	39	55	61
NEW MEXICO	585	-	-	-	-	-	-	-	01	05	09	12	18	26	30	38	44	50	58	66	78	88	94	08	13	19	23	25	27
GUAM,	586	-	***	-	-	-	01	01	01	01	01	01	03	03	03	03	03	05	05	07	07	07	09	-	-	-	-	-	-
PHILIPPINE	587	-	-	-	-	-	-	-	-	-	-	-	-	-	05	26	46	58	74	92	98	98	98	15	19	23	27	29	31
ISLANDS																													
RAILROAD	700	18	18	18	18	18	18	18	18	18	18	18	18	18	18	18	18	18	18	18	18	18	18	18	18	18	18	18	18
RETIREMENT	701	18	18	18	18	18	18	18	18	18	18	18	18	18	18	18	18	18	18	18	18	18	18	18	18	18	18	18	18
BOARD	702	18	18	18	18	18	18	18	18	18	18	18	18	18	18	18	18	18	18	18	18	18	18	18	18	18	18	18	18
	703	18	18	18	18	18	18	18	18	18	18	18	18	18	18	18	18	18	18	18	18	18	18	18	18	18	18	18	18
	704	18	18	18	18	18	18	18	18	18	18	18	18	18	18	18	18	18	18	18	18	18	18	18	18	18	18	18	18
	705	18	18	18	13	18	18	18	18	18	18	18	18	18	18	18	18	18	18	18	18	18	18	18	18	18	18	18	18
	706	18	18	18	18	18	18	18	18	18	18	18	18	18	18	18	18	18	18	18	18	18	18	18	18	18	18	18	18
	707	18	18	18	18	18	18	18	18	18	18	18	18	18	18	18	18	18	18	18	18	18	18	18	18	18	18	18	18
	708	18	18	18	18	18	18	18	18	18	18	18	18	18	18	18	18	18	18	18	18	18	18	18	18	18	18	18	18
	709	18	18	18	18	18	18	18	18	18	18	18	18	18	18	18	18	18	18	18	18	18	18	18	18	18	18	18	18
	710	18	18	18	18	18	18	18	18	18	18	18	18	18	18	18	18	18	18	18	18	18	18	18	18	18	18	18	18

CONTINUED...

Geographical and Chronological Social Security Numbers

STATE OR POSSESSION: RAILROAD RETIREMENT BOARD *(CONTINUED)*

YEAR

AREA	51	52	53	54	55	56	57	58	59	60	61	62	63	64	65	66	67	68	69	70	71	72	73	74	75	76	77	78
711	18	18	18	18	18	18	18	18	18	18	18	18	18	18	18	18	18	18	18	18	18	18	18	18	18	18	18	18
712	18	18	18	18	18	18	18	18	18	18	18	18	18	18	18	18	18	18	18	18	18	18	18	18	18	18	18	18
713	18	18	18	18	18	18	18	18	18	18	18	18	18	18	18	18	18	18	18	18	18	18	18	18	18	18	18	18
714	18	18	18	18	18	18	18	18	18	18	18	18	18	18	18	18	18	18	18	18	18	18	18	18	18	18	18	18
715	18	18	18	18	18	18	18	18	18	18	18	18	18	18	18	18	18	18	18	18	18	18	18	18	18	18	18	18
716	18	18	18	13	18	18	18	18	18	18	18	18	18	18	18	18	18	18	18	18	18	18	18	18	18	18	18	18
717	18	18	18	18	18	18	18	18	18	18	18	18	18	18	18	18	18	18	18	18	18	18	18	18	18	18	18	18
718	18	18	18	18	18	18	18	18	18	18	18	18	18	18	18	18	18	18	18	18	18	18	18	18	18	18	18	18
719	18	18	18	18	18	18	18	18	18	18	18	18	18	18	18	18	18	18	18	18	18	18	18	18	18	18	18	18
720	18	18	18	18	18	18	18	18	18	18	18	18	18	18	18	18	18	18	18	18	18	18	18	18	18	18	18	18
721	18	18	18	18	18	18	18	18	18	18	18	18	18	18	18	18	18	18	18	18	18	18	18	18	18	18	18	18
722	18	18	18	18	18	18	18	18	18	18	18	18	18	18	18	18	18	18	18	18	18	18	18	18	18	18	18	18
723	18	18	18	18	18	18	18	18	18	18	18	18	18	18	18	18	18	18	18	18	18	18	18	18	18	18	18	18
724	18	28	28	28	28	28	28	28	28	28	28	28	28	28	28	28	28	28	28	28	28	28	28	28	28	28	28	28
725	18	18	18	18	18	18	18	18	18	18	18	18	18	18	18	18	18	18	18	18	18	18	18	18	18	18	18	18
726	18	18	18	18	18	18	18	18	18	18	18	18	18	18	18	18	18	18	18	18	18	18	18	18	18	18	18	18
727	10	10	10	10	10	10	10	10	10	10	10	10	10	10	10	10	10	10	10	10	10	10	10	10	10	10	10	10
728	09	09	18	12	12	14	14	14	14	14	14	14	14	14	14	14	14	14	14	14	14	14	14	14	14	14	14	14
729	09	09	-	-	-	-	-	-	-	-	-	-	-	-	-	-	-	-	-	-	-	-	-	-	-	-	-	-
	-	-	-	-	-	-	-	-	-	-	-	-	-	-	-	-	-	-	-	-	-	-	-	-	-	-	-	-
586	-	-	-	-	-	01	01	01	01	01	03	03	03	03	03	50	05	07	07	18	07	09						
586	-	-	-	-	-	20	20	20	20	20	20	20	20	20	22	22	22	22	22	22	24	24						
586	-	-	-	-	-	30	30	30	30	30	30	30	30	30	30	30	30	30	30	30	30	30						
586	-	-	-	-	-	60	60	60	60	60	60	60	60	60	60	60	60	60	60	60	60	62	62	64	66	68	68	70

Determining The Social Security Number

5

In the last chapter we examined the information an individual's Social Security Number reveals about him or her and introduced many of the public record sources where that number can be found. There may be times when you cannot locate the SSN via public records. This could be caused by any of several factors.

Some states have very strong privacy laws that outlaw the use of Social Security Numbers on driver's licenses, voter registration cards, and other transactions not specifically mandated to use the SSN. For example, if the man you are investigating has lived in the state of Washington (which is proud of its strict privacy laws) all of his life, you will have to dig further to get his SSN. Washington state does not use SSNs on motor vehicle documents or voter registration forms, under mandate of state law.

It may also be difficult to determine the SSN of an individual who has made a deliberate choice to protect the number and keep it private. One may question the motive, but it may simply be that he values his privacy.

How then can the number be determined? Six years ago, a Federal government ruling opened up the single largest repository of Social Security Numbers and birthdates to any member of the public who wants access to this data. Who maintains this huge repository of personal information? The nation's credit bureaus.

CREDIT BUREAUS

You might be thinking that the only people who can have access to information from credit reports are credit grantors. Until 1989, that was true. But not any longer. This perhaps startling fact requires some explanation.

A credit report is composed of three main sections. The first section of the report, at the top of the page, contains identification information. This is commonly known as **header information**. Header information will contain the following data:

- FULL NAME OF INDIVIDUAL

- SOCIAL SECURITY NUMBER

- BIRTHDATE OR YEAR OF BIRTH

- CURRENT ADDRESS

- TWO PREVIOUS ADDRESSES

- CURRENT EMPLOYER

- PREVIOUS EMPLOYER

- JOB TITLE OR POSITION

The second section of the credit report contains the person's account history with his or her creditors. Each account will be listed along with the current balance, payment due, and the payment history of that account. Payment history will include such items as to how often payments were late, as well as current status of that account.

The last section of the report contains public record information. If the person has any tax liens, bankruptcies, or local court judgments outstanding, they will be posted here.

In 1989, the Federal Trade Commission (the FTC), the agency responsible for administering the laws that regulate credit bureaus, made a monumental decision. The agency decided that credit bureau header information was not credit information per se and, as such, could be released to *anyone*. Prior to that ruling, the only way any information from a credit report could be released was when a consumer had requested credit or was applying for a job or a large insurance policy.

IDENTIFICATION REPORTS

The three main credit bureaus (see *Resource List*) sell an information resource known as an "identification report" — to *anyone*. Identification reports contain this header information. Identification reports are of two varieties. These are:

- NATIONAL IDENTIFIER REPORT

- SOCIAL SECURITY TRACE REPORT

Each of these reports can be used to confirm or disprove certain facts you have been given about an individual. Let's first examine the differences between the two types of reports and when to use each one.

NATIONAL IDENTIFIER REPORTS

A **national identifier report** is used when all you have is a name and address. When this information is entered into the credit bureau computer, it will attempt to find a match in the files for the name and the address together. When it does, it will pull up the following information:

- FULL NAME

- SOCIAL SECURITY NUMBER

- BIRTHDATE

- TWO PREVIOUS ADDRESSES

- CURRENT EMPLOYER

TRACE REPORTS

A **Social Security Number trace** can be used to confirm that an SSN belongs to the particular individual. This trace will pull up the names and addresses of everyone using a particular SSN. If more than one person is using the number, it is a possible indication of someone trying to hide his or her identity.

A Social Security Number trace is activated by entering only the SSN into the files. Any file where this number has been used as an identifier will be pulled.

Information gets on header reports when a person applies for credit. If the person gave an address on a credit application, or possibly a job application, that is the same address you have, these header reports can yield good information. Header reports also can be used if you have more than one past address on an individual.

Let us assume that our subject has given you two previous addresses. You run a national identifier search on the most recent address, but get nothing. *Do not stop!* Run a second search using the older address. This second search may reveal the SSN and other vital data.

INFORMATION BROKERS

How and where does an individual do these searches? Individuals do not deal with the credit bureaus directly. Instead, they go through a third party known as an *information broker*. These are companies that link individuals, whether everyday citizens or private investigators, to providers of information. The individual makes the request via the information broker, and the broker accesses the actual database keeper via computer or fax.

A number of information brokers are very accessible to novice researchers. One of my favorites is listed below. Write or call for a copy of their current brochure. In addition to performing header searches, they also can do much of the other background work described in this book—at a price. I recommend using an information broker only for items such as header searches that are impossible for you to do on your own.

Datafax Information Services
Thomas Investigative Services
PO Box 33244
Austin, TX 78764

512-719-3595

DEATH MASTER FILE

To make sure he really is who he says he is, one other important check can be run on our mysterious subject's SSN. This search will tell us if the SSN he is using in actuality belongs to someone who has died.

The Social Security Administration's Death Master File contains over forty million Social Security Numbers that belong to deceased individuals. An SSN is entered into the Death Master File if the survivors collect the death benefit from the Social Security Administration.

How might an unscrupulous person make use of an SSN belonging to a deceased individual?

The most common use is to fraudulently re-establish credit. If a person died without ever having applied for credit with this SSN, the number could be used to start a new credit history. Such a number can be useful to a crook if the individual died recently and had a good credit history. A savvy individual could apply for credit in the deceased's name and get secondary cards issued on the account in his own name.

The Death Master File can be accessed by name, name and birthdate, Social Security Number, or first name and birthdate. A death index check will also reveal if an individual is using the SSN of a deceased relative with the same last name.

We have now seen how to verify all the different aspects of an individual's Social Security Number. We can determine if the number itself is even possible and, if so, if it has been issued. We can determine the historical basis of the number, and whether our subject is too young or too old to have it. We have seen how we can confirm the number through credit bureau records and, finally, how to make sure the number does not belong to a deceased individual. Death claim Social Security Number searches can be done efficiently via an information broker.

Once we have confirmed our subject's name, date of birth, and SSN, we can start investigating other areas of his or her life. We have learned how to check an individual's driving record and determine if any type of civil litigation is outstanding.

But does he have a criminal record? How can we find out? We'll learn the answer to that question in the next chapter.

Checking For A Criminal Record

She had finally realized her dream—a small businfess all her own. Before this, she had fifteen years of working for an aerospace firm, when the axe began to fall. After the bloodletting was over, her career had been gored along with those of thousands of others.

She used her severance payment to start a private mailbox service. It was the ideal business for her—not a lot of startup money and a ready-made clientele. But she needed to hire workers fast—workers who would accept a minimum wage job with minimal growth opportunity. She knew she could not be too picky.

The first employee was easy, a nineteen-year-old girl looking for a part-time job. Excellent references. And a local resident. The second hire was more problematical. He was 26 years old and had not been in the area long. His last employment reference was three years old and from out of state. He admitted he had been unemployed since then. She could sympathize, many of her former colleagues were still out of work. He got the job.

Everything was fine until two weeks later, when he had to close the shop. He was supposed to make the bank deposit and also prepare the transit pass receipts for pickup by the bus department. When she arrived at work the next morning, all hell broke loose.

> The bank deposit had not been made, and more than $3,000 due to the bus department was missing. She called the number listed for her new hire—no one had seen him since the day before.
>
> She had to pay the bus department out of her own pocket, and later she learned the bad news from the police. Had she done some rudimentary checking, she could have found out that her employee had stolen money from his last employer to feed his drug habit. The gap on his resumé covered up a stay in county jail for theft, armed robbery, and assault. Her money was gone for good.

The single most significant item our mystery individual might try to hide is a criminal record. Criminal record information is easy to locate once you have done the groundwork in your investigation. By now you should have a good idea as to the individual's past residences and basic identifiers, including birth date, Social Security Number, and race.

Criminal records are obtained at two levels. First, people may be convicted of violating laws of the Federal government. In this case, trials will have taken place in the Federal District Court serving the area where the defendant lived or lives. Second, local courts enforce state laws. If a state law was broken and the offender tried, the trial will have taken place in the county courthouse in the county seat where the offense occurred.

FEDERAL CRIMINAL RECORDS

We will begin with Federal criminal records because the government has made it very easy to determine if a person has had a conviction on a Federal charge.

Any person can telephone the Federal Bureau of Prisons National **Inmate Locator Service** (dial 202-307-3126) and the staff will tell you the following information about an individual who committed a Federal offense:

- ◆ WHAT HE OR SHE WAS CONVICTED OF

- ◆ WHAT PRISON(S) THE TIME WAS SERVED IN

- ◆ THE LENGTH OF THE SENTENCE

STATE CRIMINAL RECORDS

Checking on state criminal convictions is not quite so simple and easy. All states maintain a centralized database of criminal records and wanted person information. In theory, whenever a person is convicted of a crime, the local jurisdiction is supposed to forward a copy of the conviction record to the state criminal identification bureau. This information is then entered into a computer database.

The problem is that this system seldom works as it should. In most states, there are gaps in the central computer's files. Therefore, the most accurate way to check on criminal conviction information is to do a county-by-county search of each location where the subject has lived. Conviction records at the county level are public record documents and are open to the public. Almost all clerks will confirm criminal conviction information via mail.

A criminal record entry will contain the following information:

- FULL NAME

- ANY KNOWN ALIASES

- DATE OF BIRTH

- SOCIAL SECURITY NUMBER

- SEX AND RACE

- CHARGES FILED

- CONVICTION STATUS

- SENTENCE RECEIVED

To make your search truly comprehensive, you will need to search for a criminal record in neighboring counties as well. If your subject was convicted of assault in a suburb on the outskirts of the city he lives in, the record of that offense might be located in another county.

When you write to the court clerk, include the full identification of the subject, a self-addressed stamped envelope, and a money order for five dollars. Most courts charge less than this, if anything, for a criminal record check. You will usually receive a response within three to four weeks. If your subject has lived in a state that has public access to the central state crime computer, check there as well.

The states that allow public access to their centralized criminal record databases are listed next, along with directions for access and telephone numbers.

STATE CRIMINAL RECORD INFORMATION

Criminal record information will be stored at both the county court where the trial and conviction took place and in the state central crime computer. Some states allow the public access to the central computer. If a state does not appear in the following list, you will need to write to the appropriate clerk of the court in the county concerned. The states listed on the next page will also allow you to obtain criminal conviction information on any other person without a release. Federal conviction information will be available at the Federal District Court serving the area where the individual was tried.

COLORADO

Colorado Bureau of Investigation
Identification Unit
690 Kipling Street
Denver, CO 80215
303-239-4201
[Must include Full Name and Date of Birth]

DISTRICT OF COLUMBIA

District of Columbia
Criminal Records
500 Indiana Ave, NW
Washington, DC 20001
202-879-1373
[Must make request on Official State Form]

FLORIDA

Florida Department of Law Enforcement
Crime Information Bureau
PO Box 1489
Tallahassee, FL 32302
904-488-6236
[Must include Full Name, Birthdate, Race, Sex, Social Security Number, and
Previous Address]

HAWAII

Hawaii Criminal Justice Data Center
465 South King Street
Honolulu, HI 96813
808-587-3106
[Must include Name, Birthdate, SSN, Race, Sex, and SASE]

ILLINOIS

Forensic Services and Identification
260 North Chicago Street
Joliet, IL 60431
815-740-5160
[Name, Birthdate, Race, Sex, and SASE required]

INDIANA

Indiana State Police
Central Repository
100 North Senate Avenue
Indiana, IN 46204
317-232-8262
[Must make request on Official State Form]

KANSAS

`Kansas Bureau of Investigation
1620 Southwest Tyler
Topeka, KS 66612
913-296-6781
[Must make request on Official State Form]

KENTUCKY

Kentucky State Police
Records Section
1250 Louisville Rd
Frankfort, KY 40601
502-227-8713
[Full Name, Birthdate, and SSN required]

MAINE

Maine State Police
Bureau of Identification
36 Hospital Street
Augusta, ME 04330
207-624-7000
[Birthdate, Full Name, and any Aliases required]

MISSISSIPPI

Mississippi Records Department
PO Box 880
Parchman, MS 38738
601-745-6611
[Full Name, Birthdate, Race, Sex, and SSN required]

MISSOURI

Missouri State Highway Patrol
Criminal Records Division
PO Box 568
Jefferson City, MO 65102
314-751-3313
[Full Name, Race, Sex, Birthdate, and SSN required]

MONTANA

Montana Identification Bureau
303 North Roberts
Helena, MO 59620
406-444-3625
[Full Name, Race, Sex, Birthdate, and SSN required]

NORTH DAKOTA

North Dakota Bureau of Criminal Investigation
PO Box 1054
Bismarck, ND 58502
701-221-6180
[Full Name, Birthdate, and SSN required]

OKLAHOMA

Oklahoma Bureau of Investigation
Criminal History Information
PO Box 11497
Oklahoma City, OK 73136
405-427-5421
[Full Name, SSN, Race, Sex, Birthdate, and SASE required]

OREGON

Oregon State Police
Bureau of Criminal Identification
3772 Portland Road NE
Salem, OR 97310
503-378-3070
[Full Name, Birthdate, and Address required]

PENNSYLVANIA

Pennsylvania Records and Identification
Central Repository
1800 Elmerton Avenue
Harrisburg, PA 17110
717-783-5592
[Use Official Form for all requests]

SOUTH CAROLINA

South Carolina Law Enforcement Division
Criminal Records Section
PO Box 21398
Columbia, SC 29221
803-737-9000

WISCONSIN

Wisconsin Crime Information Bureau
Records Section
PO Box 2718
Madison, WI 53701
608-266-7314

This brings us to the subject of police databases. In the next chapter you will see that even in a routine traffic stop, many information banks might be consulted before you are allowed to proceed on your way. You will also see the dangers inherent in such a system, and how the liberty of the innocent may be imperiled.

In the case of our mystery person, let's say that, after carrying out this search for a criminal record, we find no record to indicate that he's a convicted felon. This part of your search is not over. Let's take a look in Chapter 7 at the information contained by police computer systems.

7

Police Computer Systems

Law enforcement agencies have a number of databases at their disposal to store and process information on private citizens. In law enforcement databases only a few appear as criminals, but almost all of us interact with the police from time to time and leave our mark.

The average individual has a first encounter with a police computer system when pulled over for a routine traffic stop. The police officer's action starts a process that results in many different files being consulted before the individual is allowed to drive away with a traffic citation or warning.

The best way to see these databanks in action is to observe a typical traffic stop from the police officer's perspective. We will assume you are driving a car, and suddenly see the flashing lights of a police car in your mirror.

While you are nervously waiting for the officer to make his appearance at your window, he is busy ascertaining information vital to his safety. Most patrol cars today have a mobile data terminal that is linked to the department's communication center. The first check made will be on your automobile license plate number. The officer wants to determine if your car has been reported stolen, if the car is suspected of involvement with criminal activity, and if the license plate information matches the vehicle.

The license plate check is accomplished via the state motor vehicle department computer. The screen on the mobile data terminal will display a menu from which the officer can choose. The switching system at the department communication center will then route the request to the correct agency mainframe computer. The motor vehicle department computer will verify that the registration of the vehicle is valid or invalid, and the details of the make, model and registered owner's name of the car.

If the car has out-of-state license plates, the department communication center will switch the request to the appropriate state motor vehicle department mainframe via the National Law Enforcement Telecommunications System. An out-of-state license check will often produce a smaller amount of information—a confirmation that the registration is valid, and the make and model of the car.

To determine if the car is stolen, the officer will check a different database. This computer system is known as the National Crime Information Center, and it is the primary law enforcement computer system in the United States. The National Crime Information Center computer is maintained by the FBI. NCIC, as it is commonly known, contains numerous files regarding people and property. One of these files contains information on all stolen vehicles.

After these checks are made, and if none of them reveals a possible dangerous situation, the officer will proceed as if this is a routine traffic stop. He will come to your window and ask to see your license and vehicle registration. After he has these documents in his hands, he will return to his patrol car, and proceed to check you and your license against several files either stored in or accessible from his mobile computer.

To understand the function of the NCIC system, we need to first understand the unique structure of policing that exists in the United States in comparison to most other nations.

Most countries have a national police force and just a few large municipal and regional forces. The United States has a long tradition of local policing. A typical metropolitan area may have many law enforcement agencies, each exercising authority in its own bailiwick (county, city, borough, local, or functional—such as public transportation).

Before the development of NCIC, a person wanted for rape could simply cross a state line, and the chances of the warrant from the old state being found during a traffic stop in the new state were very remote. NCIC eliminates this problem.

NCIC derives its effectiveness from having local police departments enter into the system all arrest warrant information, subject to a few caveats. These arrest warrants, along with those from the Federal court system, form the basis of the NCIC wanted persons file. All warrants entered into NCIC must be extradictable. Warrants for unpaid speeding tickets or parking tickets cannot be entered into NCIC.

The first file against which your license will be checked is the NCIC wanted persons index. Your full name and birthdate will be entered into the system. The response will be either "No record found," or that a possible match has been made. When a possible match is made, the warrant citation will list what the warrant is for, the department issuing the warrant, and a biography and description of the suspect.

When the officer makes a possible match with a wanted person entry, he must then call up the entire warrant entry and see if the other identifiers match before an arrest can be made. This is to avoid numerous lawsuits for false arrest. A complete wanted persons entry should contain the following information:

- FULL NAME OF SUSPECT

- ANY ALIASES USED

- DATE OF BIRTH

◆ SOCIAL SECURITY NUMBER

◆ RACE AND SEX

◆ HEIGHT AND WEIGHT

◆ EYE AND HAIR COLOR

◆ PLACE OF BIRTH

◆ DRIVER LICENSE OR ID CARD NUMBER AND STATE

◆ VEHICLE LICENSE PLATE NUMBER AND DESCRIPTION

Even though a complete entry should look like the above list, the reality is that many warrant entries are incomplete. A warrant entry can be placed into NCIC with as little as the name and year of birth. At any given time there are in excess of 400,000 wanted person warrants in the system. The danger of false arrest comes from two sources.

The first cause is that of simple keystroke error by the person entering the arrest warrant into the system. Simply misspelling a name or transposing one digit in a birthdate can cause an innocent individual to be arrested, while the real wanted person would elude a computer check. The second cause is more difficult to remedy. This happens when a person with an identical name and birthdate as your own is wanted for a crime.

This is the reason the officer must verify the other identifying information listed on the warrant entry before slapping the cuffs on you. The possibility of being falsely arrested is not an academic one. One estimate, based on warrant error rates, has determined that there are between fifteen and twenty thousand people in danger of being wrongly arrested if stopped by police.

If the arrest warrant has the same name and birthdate as you, but the rest of the warrant entry says the wanted individual is a white male with blonde hair, and you are black, you have no problem. It can get dicey if the warrant has the same name and birthdate as you, plus the same height, weight, and eye color. Then you might very well be picked up. You will be released, probably the next morning or in a few hours, after the photo and fingerprints of your namesake are received from the department originating the warrant.

If NCIC (the federal system) does not identify you as a fugitive, the officer will then check his state crime computer system. Depending upon jurisdiction, this is essentially a state level version of NCIC. The state computer system will contain those warrants that are not eligible for listing on NCIC. If you do have outstanding traffic warrants or other minor infractions, the officer will find them here.

If your license is from out of state, the patrol officer can usually check the state crime computer where your license was issued for the same information.

8

Where Was He *Really* Born?

He was an illegal immigrant, like so many millions of others in America. He knew the shadow world of false documentation in which most illegal immigrants live, with driver's licenses and Social Security cards purchased on the street—documents that would not stand careful scrutiny by police or other officials.

No, he was going to join the community—but on *his* terms. His documents would all be *real*, and he would not have to spend his life in the shadows. All he needed was a good quality false birth certificate—after that, all of his subsequent papers would be official. He knew that in our society, the birth certificate is the cornerstone upon which all other documents are based.

Our mystery man probably gave some information as to where he was born. During the course of our investigation we have developed enough identifiers to be able to obtain a copy of his birth certificate. This should be done even if we have seen an official-looking document that *purports* to be his birth record.

Millions of illegal immigrants have forged birth certificates. The use of such a document is also a time-tested way of leaving a past identity behind and starting over again. By verifying the birth record directly, we confirm in a *primary* way that he is who he purports to be. This is especially true in the case of someone who is creating a new identity, because all subsequent identification obtained with the phony birth certificate will be real.

Here's how to obtain a copy of someone's birth certificate. The mailing addresses of all state vital statistics bureaus follow. Always write or call first to get a current fee schedule before sending in a birth certificate request.

VITAL RECORDS OFFICES

Vital records are on file at two offices: the county recorder or similar office in the county or city where the birth, death, or marriage took place, or the state central vital statistics repository. The following listing is for the central vital statistics registry in each state. Before sending a document request, write or call the office and find out what the current fee is for the document you want. Make your request in a letter, or on the official form, if required. All fees should be paid via money order.

ALABAMA

State Department of Public Health
434 Monroe Street
Montgomery, AL 36130
205-261-5033

ALASKA

Bureau of Vital Statistics
P.O. Box H-02G
Juneau, AK 99811
907-465-3038

ARIZONA

Vital Records Section
P.O. Box 3887
Phoenix, AZ 85030
602-258-6381

ARKANSAS

Division of Vital Records
4815 West Targetham Street
Little Rock, AR 72201
502-445-2684

CALIFORNIA

Vital Statistics
410 N Street
Sacramento, CA 95814
916-445-2684

COLORADO

Vital Records Section
4210 East 11th Avenue
Denver, CO 80220
303-756-4464

CONNECTICUT

Vital Records
550 Main Street
Hartford, CT 06103
860-543-8538

DELAWARE

Office of Vital Statistics
P.O. Box 637
Wilmington, DE
302-739-4721

DISTRICT OF COLUMBIA

Vital Records Office
4251 I Street NW
Washington, DC 20001
202-727-5314

FLORIDA

Office of Vital Statistics
P.O. Box 210
Jacksonville, FL 32231
904-359-6000

GEORGIA

Vital Records Unit, Room 217-H
47 Trinity Avenue Southwest
Atlanta, GA 30334
404-656-7456

HAWAII

Vital Records
P.O. Box 3378
Honolulu, HI 96801
808-586-4533

IDAHO

Vital Statistics
Statehouse
Boise, ID 83720
208-334-5988

ILLINOIS

Division of Vital Records
605 West Jefferson Street
Springfield, IL 62702
217-782-6533

INDIANA

Division of Vital Records
P.O. Box 1964
Indianapolis, IN 46206
317-633-0276

IOWA

Vital Records Section
Lucas State Office Building
Des Moines, IO 50319
515-281-4944

KANSAS

Bureau of Vital Statistics
900 Southwest Jackson
Topeka, KS 66612
913-296-1400

KENTUCKY

Office of Vital Statistics
275 East Main Street
Frankfort, KY 40621
502-564-4212

LOUISIANA

Department of Vital Records
P.O. Box 60630
New Orleans, LA 70160
504-568-2561

MAINE

Office of Vital Records
State House, Station 11
Augusta, ME 04333
207-289-3184

MARYLAND

Division of Vital Records
P.O. Box 68760
Baltimore, MD 21215
410-225-5988

MASSACHUSETTS

Registry of Vital Records
150 Tremont Street
Boston, MA 02111
617-727-0110

MICHIGAN

Office of The State Registrar
P.O. Box 30195
Lansing, MI 48909
517-335-8656

MINNESOTA

Vital Statistics Section
717 Delaware Street Southeast
Minneapolis, MN 55440
612-623-5120

MISSISSIPPI

Vital Records
P.O. Box 1700
Jackson, MI 39215
601-960-7981

MISSOURI

Bureau of Vital Records
P.O. Box 570
Jefferson City, MO 65102
314-751-6400

MONTANA

Bureau of Records and Statistics
State Department of Health
Helena, MN 59620
406-444-2614

NEBRASKA

Bureau of Vital Statistics
301 Centennial Mall South
Lincoln, NE 68509
402-471-2871

NEVADA

Vital Statistics
505 East King Street
Carson City, NV 89710
702-885-4480

NEW JERSEY

State Department of Health
Bureau of Vital Statistics, CN-370
Trenton, NJ 08625
609-292-4087

NEW MEXICO

Vital Statistics Bureau
1190 Saint Francis Drive
Santa Fe, NM 87504
505-827-0121

NEW YORK

Bureau of Vital Statistics
Department of Health
125 Worth Street
New York, NY 10013
212-619-4530

NORTH CAROLINA

Vital Records Section
P.O. Box 27687
Raleigh, NC 27611
919-733-3526

NORTH DAKOTA

Division of Vital Records
State Department of Health
Bismark, ND 58505
701-224-2360

OHIO

Bureau of Vital Statistics
246 North High Street
Columbus, OH 43215
614-466-2531

OKLAHOMA

Vital Records Section
P.O. Box 53551
Oklahoma City, OK 73152
405-271-4108

OREGON

Vital Statistics Section
P.O. Box 14050
Portland, OR 97214
503-731-4108

PENNSYLVANIA

Division of Vital Statistics
P.O. Box 1528
New Castle, PA 16103
412-656-3100

RHODE ISLAND

Division of Vital Statistics
Cannon Building
3 Capitol Hill
Providence, RI 02908
401-277-2811

SOUTH CAROLINA

Vital Records
2600 Bull Street
Columbia, SC 29201
803-734-4830

SOUTH DAKOTA

Vital Records Program
523 East Capital
Pierre, SD 57501
605-773-4963

TENNESSEE

Tennessee Vital Records
Cordell Hull Office Building
Nashville, TN 37247
615-741-1763

TEXAS

Bureau of Vital Records
1100 West 49th Street
Austin, TX 78756
512-458-7364

UTAH

Bureau of Vital Records
P.O. Box 1670
Salt Lake City, UT 84116
801-538-6380

VERMONT

Vital Records Section
Box 70, 60 Main Street
Burlington, VT 05402
802-863-7271

VIRGINIA

Bureau of Vital Records
P.O. Box 1000
Richmond, VA 23208
804-786-6228

WASHINGTON

Center of Health Statistics
P.O. Box 9709
Olympia, WA 98507
306-753-6936

WEST VIRGINIA

Vital Registration Office
State Capitol Complex
Charleston, WV 25305
304-558-2931

WISCONSIN

Bureau of Health Records
P.O. Box 309
Madison, WI 53701
608-266-1371

WYOMING

Vital Records
Hathaway Building
Cheyenne, WY 82002
307-777-7591

9

Employment, Educational, and Financial Records

The job applicant's resumé was impressive. She had a master's degree in Finance from a major university and excellent letters of reference from former employers. Her university transcripts revealed a 3.8 grade point average.

The head of personnel called the last employer listed on the resumé to confirm the glowing reference letter. It checked out, so he hired the woman without any more thought. A few months later he heard from her department supervisor, wondering how personnel could have hired such an incompetent worker.

Perplexed, he checked out the woman again, this time calling all of the references and calling the university directly. The whole resumé proved to be a sham, and the woman was fired the same day.

So far in our investigation we have focused on determining what our mystery man (or woman) is not. He is not a convicted felon. He is not a person with a bad driving record. He is not the subject of lawsuits. We have confirmed that his Social Security Number is valid and probably belongs to him, and that he was born where he said he was.

But what has he done with his life? Is he an educated man or an individual of modest academic achievement? Is he a wealthy person who hides his assets and keeps a low profile? Is he a reliable worker, or does he collect worker's compensation payments habitually?

Let's look first at a wealthy individual who pretends he is not. There is a type of investigative tool that can be very useful in determining what a celebrity owns, or whether a politician who claims to be a common working man is really a multimillionaire.

CORPORATE SHELLS

We have seen earlier that, if you own property or automobiles in your own name, the public can learn this very quickly. Many wealthy individuals or people worried about lawsuits avoid having property or vehicles in their own names by using a corporate shell to acquire these assets. An assets search in their name would reveal nothing, because the corporation owns everything.

The key, therefore, is to determine if the subject has any corporations registered in his name. Once you know the name of the corporation, you can then search for real assets registered to the company and, by proxy, to him.

It is easy to check out a corporation. Each state has a Secretary of State Office, which ensures unique corporation names and registers the articles of incorporation for all companies incorporated within that state. Incorporation papers are public record documents that may provide valuable information about the subject.

At the end of this chapter are the Secretary of State Office addresses for each state. Write to these offices to determine if a corporation exists in the name of your subject.

BUSINESS CREDIT REPORTS

Once you have the information from the Secretary of State, you can then pull a **business credit report** on the company via an information broker. Such reports can be ordered by anyone. You may find out that although your subject has no debts or major assets in his own name, the company he owns might be on the slippery slope to bankruptcy, or very wealthy.

UCC FILINGS

The Secretary of State can also provide you with what are known as **Universal Commercial Code** (UCC) filings. A UCC filing allows a creditor to secure his interest in items purchased on credit by individuals or companies. In many states, these can be found at the state level. If a UCC search reveals a filing under your subject's name, order a copy of the entire document. A UCC filing will usually contain the following information:

- ◆ NAME OF BANK OR FINANCIAL INSTITUTION

- ◆ ANY COLLATERAL USED TO SECURE LOAN

- ◆ NAME OF ANY COSIGNERS

- ◆ FULL NAME AND ADDRESS OF BORROWERS

- ◆ ADDRESS OF BANK OR FINANCIAL INSTITUTION

EDUCATION RECORDS

Education records should be verified directly with the schools concerned. Don't be impressed by a diploma on the wall or a genuine looking transcript. Millions of people use fake or inflated credentials to get jobs for which they are not formally qualified. With the information you now have, you can verify in depth your subject's educational background.

The first aspect of educational background you may wish to confirm is the university attended and the degree earned. In most cases, this is easy to do using two avenues.

Most colleges will release a fair amount of student information over the telephone or by mail to anyone. The only time this won't be done is when a student has made a privacy request, asking that the college divulge information only with his or her prior approval. What kinds of information can you obtain in this informal fashion? The following items are often available:

- ◆ FULL NAME OF STUDENT

- ◆ DATES ATTENDED

- ◆ MAJOR

- ◆ DEGREES RECEIVED

- ◆ HONORS OR AWARDS

- ◆ LOCAL ADDRESS

- ◆ HOME ADDRESS

A check of college records may reveal a past address your subject did not speak of, or might reveal a discrepancy between his claimed achievements and reality. This informal check is fine as far as it goes, but you may want more information. You can only be absolutely positive of his accomplishments if you order a copy of his **academic transcript** directly from the school.

ACADEMIC TRANSCRIPTS

Transcripts are usually released only to the student or a prospective employer or graduate school. You have enough information to request transcripts by writing for them in his name.

To request college transcripts, you will need to give some combination of the following information in your letter to the college:

♦ FULL NAME

♦ SOCIAL SECURITY NUMBER

♦ DATES OF ENROLLMENT

♦ MAJOR

The transcripts will confirm your subject's actual academic achievement and degree status. Once you have done this, you will want to verify his employment background.

EMPLOYMENT RECORDS

Due to liability and privacy laws, it's usually difficult to get a human resources or admin person to provide more than "yes, he worked here" even to formal inquiries from prospective new employers. But there's a better way called "human engineering." Call the company and determine who else works in the department where your subject was likely employed. After a couple of calls, you should have some idea of who does what, and who the subject's co-workers were/are. If you can contact them informally, they might be much more open regarding the information you're seeking.

Many occupations are regulated at the state and local levels via a licensing process. Most people know that doctors and school teachers are licensed by the state, but so are many other professions. When an occupation is licensed, the licensing records are open for public inspection. Licensing records can also sometimes turn up potential problems that a criminal conviction check will not reveal.

Suppose our subject is a physician with a history of abusing his prescription privileges. The state medical board may have censured him or given him a temporary license suspension a few years ago. This would not come up on a criminal record check because the state or county medical board would have handled it.

The same type of problem can exist with people who once were, or are, child care workers or school teachers. Perhaps he told you he was a teacher years ago, but no longer works with children. Was it really just a case of changing careers, or did he lose his license based on allegations of ethics violations, or unprofessional contact with a child?

The license status of physicians can be checked with the state or county medical board. Attorneys' professional standing can be ascertained via the county bar association. All state education departments will confirm a school teacher's license.

Anyone who works as a pilot, aircraft mechanic, air traffic controller, or flight dispatcher, will have a federal license issued by the Federal Aviation Administration. A name and birthdate, or name and Social Security Number, is usually enough to do a search.

The address is:

Federal Aviation Administration
P.O. Box 25082
AAC-260
Oklahoma City, OK 73125

Other occupations that are typically licensed at either the state or local level include the following:

- AUTO MECHANICS

- BARBERS

- BILL COLLECTORS

- BUILDING CONTRACTORS

- BURGLAR ALARM INSTALLERS

- CARPENTERS

- DOG AND CAT GROOMERS

- EXTERMINATORS

- HAIR STYLISTS

- MEDICAL TECHNICIANS AND THERAPISTS

- NOTARIES PUBLIC

- PHARMACISTS

- REAL ESTATE AGENTS

- SECURITY GUARDS

- STOCKBROKERS

- VETERINARIANS

Some of these occupations will be regulated by specialized state boards—a state board of pharmacy, for example. Information on an occupational license can be obtained by writing to the Secretary of State's office and finding out if that occupation is licensed in the state. A nationwide list of Secretaries of State begins on the following page.

SECRETARIES OF STATE OFFICE LISTINGS

ALABAMA

Corporations Division
Office of The Secretary of State
P.O. Box 5616
Montgomery, AL 36103

ALASKA

Division of Corporations
P.O. Box 110807
Juneau, AK 99811

ARIZONA

Arizona Corporation Commission
Secretary of State
1200 West Washington
Phoenix, AZ 85005

ARKANSAS

Corporations Department
Secretary of State Office
State Capitol
Little Rock, AR 72201

CALIFORNIA

Corporate Division
Secretary of State
1230 J Street
Sacramento, CA 95814

COLORADO

Department of State
1560 Broadway
Denver, CO 80202

CONNECTICUT

Office of The Secretary of State
30 Trinity Street
Hartford, CT 06106

DELAWARE

Division of Corporations
P.O. Box 793
Dover, DE 19903

DISTRICT OF COLUMBIA

Deeds Office
Sixth and D Street, NW
Washington, D.C. 20001

FLORIDA

Division of Corporations
Post Office Box 6327
Tallahassee, FL 32301

GEORGIA

Secretary of State
2 Martin Luther King Drive, SE
Atlanta, GA 30034

HAWAII

Corporations Department
1010 Richards Street
Honolulu, HI 96813

IDAHO

Secretary of State
Statehouse Room 203
Boise, ID 83720

ILLINOIS

Office of The Secretary
Centennial Bldg, Room 328
Springfield, IL 62756

INDIANA

Secretary of State
Statehouse, Room 155
Indianapolis, IN 46204

IOWA

Secretary of State
14th And Walnut Streets
Des Moines, IA 50319

KANSAS

Secretary of State
Statehouse, Room 200
Topeka, KS 66612

KENTUCKY

Secretary of State
P.O. Box 718
Frankfort, KY 40602

LOUISIANA

Department of State
P.O. Box 94125
Baton Rouge, LA 70804

MAINE

Secretary of State
Statehouse, Station 101
Augusta, ME 04333

MARYLAND

Department of Corporations
301 West Preston Street
Baltimore, MD 21201

MASSACHUSETTS

Secretary of The Commonwealth
One Ashburton Place
Boston, MA 02133

MICHIGAN

Corporations Division
6546 Mercantile Drive
Lansing, MI 48909

MINNESOTA

Secretary of State
State Office Building Room 180
St. Paul, MN 55155

MISSISSIPPI

Secretary of State
P.O. Box 136
Jackson, MS 39205

MISSOURI

Office of The Secretary of State
P.O. Box 1159
Jefferson City, MO 65101

MONTANA

Secretary of State
State Capitol
Helena, MT 59620

NEBRASKA

Secretary of State
301 Centennial Mall South
Lincoln, NE 68509

NEVADA

Secretary of State
Capitol Complex
Carson City, NV 89710

NEW HAMPSHIRE

Secretary of State
Statehouse Annex
Concord, NH 03301

NEW JERSEY

Secretary of State
Statehouse
Trenton, NJ 08625

NEW MEXICO

Secretary of State
State Office Building
Santa Fe, NM 87503

NEW YORK

Department of State
162 Washington Avenue
Albany, NY 12231

NORTH CAROLINA

Secretary of State
300 North Salisbury
Raleigh, NC 27611

NORTH DAKOTA

Secretary of State
601 East Boulevard Avenue
Bismarck, ND 58501

OHIO

Secretary of State
50 East Broad Street
Columbus, OH 43215

OKLAHOMA

Secretary of State
State Capitol Building
Oklahoma City, OK 73105

OREGON

Department of Commerce
158 12th NE
Salem, OR 97310

PENNSYLVANIA

Secretary of State
North Office Building
Harrisburg, PA 17120

RHODE ISLAND

Secretary of State
Corporations Division
270 Westminster Mall
Providence, RI 02903

SOUTH CAROLINA

Secretary of State
P.O. Box 11350
Columbia, SC 29211

SOUTH DAKOTA

Secretary of State
500 East Capitol
Pierre, SD 57501

TENNESSEE

Secretary of State
James K. Polk Building
Nashville, TN 37219

TEXAS

Secretary of State
P.O. Box 13193
Austin, TX 78711

UTAH

Secretary of State
160 East Third Street
Salt Lake City, UT 84145

VERMONT

Secretary of State
109 State Street
Montpelier, VT 05602

VIRGINIA

Secretary of State
P.O. Box 1197
Richmond, VA 23209

WASHINGTON

Secretary of State
211 12th Street
Olympia, WA 98504

WISCONSIN

Secretary of State
P.O. Box 7648
Madison, WI 53707

WYOMING

Secretary of State
110 Capitol Building
Cheyenne, WY 82002

If the individual's profession is licensed, you can order a copy of the licensing file and history. You will probably receive some combination of the following data:

- ◆ FULL NAME ON LICENSE
- ◆ WORK ADDRESS AT TIME OF LICENSING
- ◆ HOME ADDRESS AT TIME OF LICENSING
- ◆ LICENSE NUMBER
- ◆ LENGTH OF TIME LICENSE HELD
- ◆ SCHOOLS ATTENDED
- ◆ BIRTHDATE
- ◆ COMPLAINT HISTORY

10

Was He *Really* In The Military?

He had regaled her with many fascinating stories of his 20-year military career. Numerous plaques, certificates, and commendations lined the wall of his study. He had enlisted right out of high school, and was now starting a second career at the age of 38. He frequently talked about the benefits of military retirement, and the fact that you kept your PX, commissary, and military health-care privileges after leaving the service.

Her father, who was also a retired military man, decided to invite his daughter and new boyfriend out for dinner at the NCO club at a local army base. The house of cards all came tumbling down when the boyfriend could not enter the base because he did not have an Armed Forces Identification Card—the *one* document a real retiree would always carry. He wasn't even a competent fraud, since a fake card will usually pass casual scrutiny.

Many people claim to have served in the military. Veterans are looked upon with favor by civilian employers because servicemen are usually disciplined individuals with a good work ethic. Anyone who can survive basic training and obtain an honorable discharge has proven himself in ways most have not.

VETERANS

Veterans receive all sorts of benefits once they leave the service. Depending upon individual circumstances, these include free medical care at Veterans Administration hospitals around the country, educational benefits, special low cost mortgage opportunities, and even burial rights. Retired veterans (and their families) are even entitled to lifetime access to military bases and the commissaries, exchanges, pharmacies, and military hospitals contained within.

A person leaves the military in one of two statuses (discharged or retired). He may serve only his enlistment contract, or as an officer for a contractual number of years, and then be discharged or released from active duty. These individuals have official status as veterans, and their benefits are provided by the Department of Veterans Affairs. They are issued discharge certificates by the branch of the service they were in and also receive a plastic Veterans Affairs identification card with their name and Social Security Number on it.

Veterans, with few exceptions, no longer carry armed forces identification documents, and do not have routine access to military bases after discharge.

RETIREES

The second set of former service members are retirees, who leave the service with more than 19.5 years of duty, and receive 2.5% of their service salary for the remainder of their lives. Military retirees continue to carry armed forces identification documents and have continued access to base facilities. Retirees may go to military hospitals for medical care and have commissary and exchange privileges after retirement. Commissioned officers retain their commissions, albeit in a different status. A retired officer still has a commission from the United States and, under certain (unlikely) circumstances, can be recalled.

MILITARY SERVICE RECORDS

Our subject may have all sorts of certificates and service medals on display. These accoutrements cannot be taken as a definitive statement of prior service. Why not? The sad fact is that there is a big business in the manufacture and sale of bogus military certificates, identification cards, and medals. Anyone can purchase medals, uniforms, and official-looking armed forces papers. To ascertain if an individual *was* truly in the military, or really *is* currently in the service, you must verify this information with the military directly.

Fortunately, military service records are public information. Service members are paid with tax money, hence their duty records are generally available to the public. You might wonder why an individual would falsely claim to have served in the military. Aside from being more favorably considered by employers, there may be a more devious reason.

An individual who served a prison term may choose to fabricate a military tour to account for time behind bars. Employers almost always accept without question the discharge papers veterans present when seeking work. After a four-year stint in the military, an honorable discharge will usually be all the documentation an employer requires of a veteran. The employer may ask for details about some of the individual's training, duty assignments, and jobs performed, but deeper checking is not usual.

A fraud will often be well-prepared, with stories, unit designations, certificates, medals/ribbons, and perhaps even scars attributed to wounds inflicted during some heroic event. The only valid way to check is to obtain information from an independent source, the government. Even then, it's critical that the identity about which you're inquiring really belongs to the person you're checking.

You can obtain the military service record of an current or former military member by making a request on a **Form 180**, which is reproduced at the end of this chapter. The request must be made on this form if it is to be processed reliably. If a request is *made any other way*, it may lie unprocessed for many months, or will be ignored entirely.

A military service record will contain at least the following information:

- FULL NAME OF SERVICE MEMBER

- BIRTHDATE

- SERVICE NUMBER

- DATES OF SERVICE

- DUTY ASSIGNMENTS

- PROMOTIONS AND CITATIONS

- SPECIAL SERVICE SCHOOLS ATTENDED

- PAY AND ALLOWANCES RECEIVED

The second key to obtaining military records quickly is to send your request to the correct address. The various addresses are given on the second page of Form 180, but some explanation will help.

In general, people who served on active duty in one of the armed forces, and then were discharged or retired, will have their service records sent six months later to the National Personnel Records Center in St. Louis. This record center also contains the records of those who served in the reserves or National Guard, and who have since retired or been discharged from those service components.

Persons on active duty will have their service records kept at the repository for active enlisted or officers by each service. Look at the form carefully to determine which address to which the request should be sent.

Active reservists— so called Weekend Warriors—will usually have their records kept at a separate location identified on the Form 180.

Active National Guard members are a special case. The Air and Army National Guards of each state are under the control of the governor of the particular state, unless the President federalizes them (typically in an emergency). The records of active National Guard members are usually kept by the Adjutant General in the state capitol.

The key to determining if a person was really in the military requires that you have accurate answers to the following questions before you use Form 180.

These requirements are:

- ♦ WHAT BRANCH OF THE SERVICE WAS HE OR SHE IN?

- ♦ WAS HE OR SHE A RESERVIST, GUARDSMAN, OR ON ACTIVE DUTY?

- ♦ WHAT YEARS OF SERVICE ARE CLAIMED?

- ♦ WHAT AWARDS AND CITATIONS ARE CLAIMED?

- ♦ DOES THE SUBJECT HAVE A VETERANS IDENTIFICATION CARD?

- ♦ WHAT IS THE FULL NAME AND BIRTHDATE?

When you can answer these questions, you are ready to make use of Form 180. Do not be put off by the official sounding restrictions cited on the form. *Service records are public and must be released to those who request them.*

REQUEST PERTAINING TO MILITARY RECORDS

Please read instructions on the reverse. If more space is needed, use plain paper.

PRIVACY ACT OF 1974 COMPLIANCE INFORMATION. The following information is provided in accordance with 5 U.S.C. 552a(e)(3) and applies to this form. Authority for collection of the information is 44 U.S.C. 2907, 3101, and 3103, and E.O. 9397 of November 22, 1943. Disclosure of the information is voluntary. The principal purpose of the information is to assist the facility servicing the records in locating and verifying the correctness of the requested records or information to answer your inquiry. Routine uses of the information as established and published in accordance with 5 U.S.C.a(e)(4)(D)

include the transfer of relevant information to appropriate Federal, State, local, or foreign agencies for use in civil, criminal, or regulatory investigations or prosecution. In addition, this form will be filed with the appropriate military records and may be transferred along with the record to another agency in accordance with the routine uses established by the agency which maintains the record. If the requested information is not provided, it may not be possible to service your inquiry.

SECTION I—INFORMATION NEEDED TO LOCATE RECORDS (Furnish as much as possible)

1. NAME USED DURING SERVICE *(Last, first, and middle)*	2. SOCIAL SECURITY NO.	3. DATE OF BIRTH	4. PLACE OF BIRTH

5. ACTIVE SERVICE, PAST AND PRESENT (For an effective records search, it is important that ALL service be shown below)

BRANCH OF SERVICE *(Also, show last organization, if known)*	DATES OF ACTIVE SERVICE		Check one		SERVICE NUMBER DURING THIS PERIOD
	DATE ENTERED	DATE RELEASED	OFFI-CER	EN-LISTED	

6. RESERVE SERVICE, PAST OR PRESENT   If "none," check here ▶ ☐

a. BRANCH OF SERVICE	b. DATES OF MEMBERSHIP		c. Check one		d. SERVICE NUMBER DURING THIS PERIOD
	FROM	TO	OFFI-CER ☐	EN-LISTED ☐	

7. NATIONAL GUARD MEMBERSHIP *(Check one):*   a. ARMY ☐   b. AIR FORCE ☐   c. NONE ☐

d. STATE	e. ORGANIZATION	f. DATES OF MEMBERSHIP		g. Check one		h. SERVICE NUMBER DURING THIS PERIOD
		FROM	TO	OFFI-CER ☐	EN-LISTED ☐	

8. IS SERVICE PERSON DECEASED   ☐ YES   ☐ NO   If "yes," enter date of death.   **9. IS (WAS) INDIVIDUAL A MILITARY RETIREE OR FLEET RESERVIST**   ☐ YES   ☐ NO

SECTION II—REQUEST

1. EXPLAIN WHAT INFORMATION OR DOCUMENTS YOU NEED; OR, CHECK ITEM 2; OR, COMPLETE ITEM 3

2. IF YOU ONLY NEED A STATEMENT OF SERVICE *check here* ☐

3. LOST SEPARATION DOCUMENT REPLACEMENT REQUEST *(Complete a or b, and c.)*

☐	a. REPORT OF SEPARATION *(DD Form 214 or equivalent)*	YEAR ISSUED	This contains information normally needed to determine eligibility for benefits. It may be furnished only to the veteran, the surviving next of kin, or to a representative with veteran's signed release *(item 5 of this form)*.
☐	b. DISCHARGE CERTIFICATE	YEAR ISSUED	This shows only the date and character at discharge. It is of little value in determining eligibility for benefits. It may be issued only to veterans discharged honorably or under honorable conditions; or, if deceased, to the surviving spouse.

c. EXPLAIN HOW SEPARATION DOCUMENT WAS LOST

4. EXPLAIN PURPOSE FOR WHICH INFORMATION OR DOCUMENTS ARE NEEDED

6. REQUESTER

a. IDENTIFICATION *(check appropriate box)*

☐ Same person identified in Section I   ☐ Surviving spouse

☐ Next of kin (relationship) _____

☐ Other (specify)

b. SIGNATURE *(see instruction 3 on reverse side)*   DATE OF REQUEST

5. RELEASE AUTHORIZATION, IF REQUIRED *(Read instruction 3 on reverse side)*

I hereby authorize release of the requested information/documents to the person indicated at right (item 7).

VETERAN SIGN HERE ▶ _____

(If signed by other than veteran show relationship to veteran.)

7. *Please type or print clearly —*   COMPLETE RETURN ADDRESS

Name, number and street, city, State and ZIP code

TELEPHONE NO. *(Include area code)* ▶

INSTRUCTIONS

1. Information needed to locate records. Certain identifying information is necessary to determine the location of an individual's record of military service. Please give careful consideration to and answer each item on this form. If you do not have and cannot obtain the information for an item, show "NA," meaning the information is "not available." Include as much of the requested information as you can. This will help us to give you the best possible service.

2. Charges for service. A nominal fee is charged for certain types of service. In most instances service fees cannot be determined in advance. If your request involves a service fee you will be notified as soon as that determination is made.

3. Restrictions on release of information. Information from records of military personnel is released subject to restrictions imposed by the military departments consistent with the provisions of the Freedom of Information Act of 1967 (as amended in 1974) and the Privacy Act of 1974. A service person has access to almost any information contained in his own record. The next of kin, if the veteran is deceased, and Federal officers for official purposes, are authorized to receive information from a military service or medical record only as specified in the above cited Acts. Other requesters must have the release authorization, in item 5 of the form, signed by the veteran or, if deceased, by the next of kin. Employers

and others needing proof of military service are expected to accept the information shown on documents issued by the Armed Forces at the time a service person is separated.

4. Location of military personnel records. The various categories of military personnel records are described in the chart below. For each category there is a code number which indicates the address at the bottom of the page to which this request should be sent. For each military service there is a note explaining approximately how long the records are held by the military service before they are transferred to the National Personnel Records Center, St. Louis. Please read these notes carefully and make sure you send your inquiry to the right address. Please note especially that the record is not sent to the National Personnel Records Center as long as the person retains any sort of reserve obligation, whether drilling or non-drilling.
(If the person has two or more periods of service within the same branch, send your request to the office having the record for the last period of service.)

5. Definitions for abbreviations used below:
NPRC — National Personnel Records Center   PERS — Personnel Records
TDRL — Temporary Disability Retirement List   MED — Medical Records

SERVICE	NOTE: (See paragraph 4 above.)	CATEGORY OF RECORDS — WHERE TO WRITE ADDRESS CODE		▼
AIR FORCE (USAF)	*Except for TDRL and general officers retired with pay, Air Force records are transferred to NPRC from Code 1, 90 days after separation and from Code 2, 150 days after separation.*	Active members (includes National Guard on active duty in the Air Force), TDRL, and general officers retired with pay.		1
		Reserve, retired reservist in nonpay status, current National Guard officers not on active duty in Air Force, and National Guard released from active duty in Air Force.		2
		Current National Guard enlisted not on active duty in Air Force.		13
		Discharged, deceased, and retired with pay.		14
COAST GUARD (USCG)	*Coast Guard officer and enlisted records are transferred to NPRC 7 months after separation.*	Active, reserve, and TDRL members.		3
		Discharged, deceased, and retired members *(see next item)*.		14
		Officers separated before 1/1/29 and enlisted personnel separated before 1/1/15.		6
MARINE CORPS (USMC)	*Marine Corps records are transferred to NPRC between 6 and 9 months after separation.*	Active, TDRL, and Selected Marine Corps Reserve members.		4
		Individual Ready Reserve and Fleet Marine Corps Reserve members.		5
		Discharged, deceased, and retired members *(see next item)*.		14
		Members separated before 1/1/1905.		6
ARMY (USA)	*Army records are transferred to NPRC as follows: Active Army and Individual Ready Reserve Control Groups: About 60 days after separation. U.S. Army Reserve Troop Unit personnel: About 120 to 180 days after separation.*	Reserve, living retired members, retired general officers, and active duty records of current National Guard members who performed service in the U.S. Army before 7/1/72.*		7
		Active officers (including National Guard on active duty in the U.S. Army).		8
		Active enlisted (including National Guard on active duty in the U.S. Army) and enlisted TDRL.		9
		Current National Guard officers not on active duty in the U.S. Army.		12
		Current National Guard enlisted not on active duty in the U.S. Army.		13
		Discharged and deceased members *(see next item)*.		14
		Officers separated before 7/1/17 and enlisted separated before 11/1/12.		6
		Officers and warrant officers TDRL.		8
NAVY (USN)	*Navy records are transferred to NPRC 6 months after retirement or complete separation.*	Active members (including reservists on duty) — PERS and MED		10
		Discharged, deceased, retired (with and without pay) less than six months, TDRL, drilling and nondrilling reservists	PERS ONLY	10
			MED ONLY	11
		Discharged, deceased, retired (with and without pay) more than six months *(see next item)* — PERS & MED		14
		Officers separated before 1/1/03 and enlisted separated before 1/1/1886 — PERS and MED		6

*Code 12 applies to active duty records of current National Guard officers who performed service in the U.S. Army after 6/30/72.
Code 13 applies to active duty records of current National Guard enlisted members who performed service in the U.S. Army after 6/30/72.

	ADDRESS LIST OF CUSTODIANS (BY CODE NUMBERS SHOWN ABOVE) — Where to write / send this form for each category of records						
1	Air Force Manpower and Personnel Center Military Personnel Records Division Randolph AFB, TX 78150-6001	**5**	Marine Corps Reserve Support Center 10950 El Monte Overland Park, KS 66211-1408	**8**	USA MILPERCEN ATTN: DAPC-MSR 200 Stovall Street Alexandria, VA 22332-0400	**12**	Army National Guard Personnel Center Columbia Pike Office Building 5600 Columbia Pike Falls Church, VA 22041
2	Air Reserve Personnel Center Denver, CO 80280-5000	**6**	Military Archives Division National Archives and Records Administration Washington, DC 20408	**9**	Commander U.S. Army Enlisted Records and Evaluation Center Ft. Benjamin Harrison, IN 46249-5301	**13**	The Adjutant General *(of the appropriate State, DC, or Puerto Rico)*
3	Commandant U.S. Coast Guard Washington, DC 20593-0001	**7**	Commander U.S. Army Reserve Personnel Center ATTN: DARP-PAS 9700 Page Boulevard St. Louis, MO 63132-5200	**10**	Commander Naval Military Personnel Command ATTN: NMPC-036 Washington, DC 20370-5036	**14**	National Personnel Records Center (Military Personnel Records) 9700 Page Boulevard St. Louis, MO 63132
4	Commandant of the Marine Corps (Code MMRB-10) Headquarters, U.S. Marine Corps Washington, DC 20380-0001			**11**	Naval Reserve Personnel Center New Orleans, LA 70146-5000		

11

You've Got Credit, But Does He or She?

They had just gotten married and were embarking on their new life together. He was a young engineer, fresh out of college, ready to take his first job. She was a few years older, but she was a good person, and he loved her to distraction.

They moved to California and applied to rent their first apartment together. The rental application was very detailed, and requested lots of information about both of them. He thought nothing of it.

A few days later, the prospective landlord called, and said their rental application was rejected. The landlord said his credit was fine, but his bride's credit history was so bad that the company could not rent them the apartment.

A person without the ability to obtain credit is an all too familiar result of today's unstable job market. People who have made plans based on a steady job can find themselves in the poorhouse quickly if that job vanishes in a corporate restructuring or downsizing. What I am saying is that bad credit, in and of itself, cannot be used to make a character judgment about an individual.

But our concern with bad credit has a different motivation. In the process of backgrounding our young, or not so young, man or woman, certain representations have been made to us about that individual's past. By now, we should know if he or she has been unemployed for extended periods of time in the past or has suffered some other major financial setback. If the subject has not indicated that either has happened, it would be only natural to expect that this person has established a credit history. Most importantly, it should be a *good* credit history.

All of our previous record checking will not reveal a bad credit history unless it uncovered a bankruptcy filing or creditor lawsuits. If the credit is bad due to financial mismanagement, but was just written off by the creditors, we can only find this out by obtaining the individual's credit report.

The methods we are about to discuss are *totally illegal when done without the consent of the subject*, and I cannot recommend that you employ them. That having been said, I can tell you that many investigators frequently use such questionable practices when checking out an individual's background.

One method involves applying for some type of credit in the subject's name and then seeing if the application is approved or denied. The *reasons* for denial are very important. The fact to remember here is that you are not actually interested in obtaining credit in the subject's name, merely in ascertaining whether a credit application will be approved. How then do you go about this? Two methods are frequently employed.

The first is the **used car shopper method**. Some auto dealers will run an individual's credit report provided over the telephone to prequalify an applicant before he or she even visits the lot. This is especially true when a big sale is in process. The would-be used car buyer gives a sales representative the necessary personal information over the telephone, and is put on hold.

The credit manager runs the credit bureau report on the computer and gives the salesman a yes or no right then and there. If your credit is good, you will be invited to come down to the lot. If it is bad, you will be told why and wished better luck in the future.

The second method involves **applying for instant credit over the telephone** with a credit card issuer or loan company. These companies use an automated system that will issue an approval or a decline in a few minutes while you are on the phone. Between the two methods, the first one is better, because you have not obtained any credit in the subject's name.

If you use the second method and an approval is received, make up a plausible reason why you do not want the card right away. Under the credit laws, you have that right. The creditor will cancel the account, and the card will not be sent.

If the application is *declined*, ask why and find out the reason in as much detail as possible. If the credit manager says there is just one bad account on the credit report, our subject has probably been truthful about his or her financial standing. On the other hand, if the application is denied due to *insufficient credit history*, your warning sensors should be activated.

Insufficient credit history normally means that the credit report contained no credit history information. Depending on our subject's age and background, this could be an indication of a person living under a new identity. For an adult living in today's society, it is almost impossible not to have *some* credit history, good or bad, someplace.

12

Taxes and Bankruptcies

We have seen how to obtain legal records such as judgments and liens. Bankruptcy is a special case because the bankruptcy law is a Federal one with a special court to administer it. If our subject declared bankruptcy long ago (usually more than ten years), it may not show up on the current credit report.

The other type of information we may want to obtain is tax information. Some tax information is publicly available, other tax information is not, but can be obtained through methods that are *illegal*. Let's look at bankruptcy information first.

BANKRUPTCY

Millions of people go bankrupt every year in the United States. The bankruptcy laws were enacted to allow individuals whose debts are unmanageable to free themselves of this millstone, and then start over fresh and debt free. Of course, there is a price to be paid for this proverbial second chance at financial life.

Creditors look upon bankruptcy as nothing short of legalized stealing. Reflecting this attitude, credit bureaus will report this negative information on the subject's credit report for ten years after the bankruptcy is filed. If our subject declared bankruptcy more than ten years ago, it *may* not show up on his credit report.

A two-stage procedure should be used to determine if our subject has declared bankruptcy. First, we should determine if he or she has ever *filed* for bankruptcy. If the answer is "yes," we will then obtain a copy of the bankruptcy file. Depending upon the state, the bankruptcy file will contain all or most of the following information:

♦ FULL NAME

♦ BIRTHDATE

♦ SOCIAL SECURITY NUMBER

♦ SPOUSE'S NAME

♦ SPOUSE'S SOCIAL SECURITY NUMBER

♦ NAMES OF ANY CHILDREN

♦ BANK ACCOUNTS AND BALANCES

♦ STOCKS AND BONDS HELD

♦ ALL PROPERTY, MOTOR VEHICLES, AND OTHER ASSETS

♦ EMPLOYMENT HISTORY

♦ SALARY AND FRINGE BENEFITS

The complete file can act as further verification of the information the subject has given you. Make a list of all the addresses at which the subject has lived. Then write the clerk of the bankruptcy court serving those various locations. In your letter you should include the subject's full name, Social Security Number, and birthdate. The clerk will confirm whether there is or is not a bankruptcy filed under this name. There should normally be no charge for this service.

If there is a filing under the subject's name and you wish to order a copy of the full file, you will need to telephone the bankruptcy court clerk and determine the cost of having the file sent to you.

An alternative method of locating bankruptcy filings is faster and makes use of the previously mentioned information brokers.

Many such brokers can make a nationwide search of bankruptcy filings. This eliminates the possibility of missing a bankruptcy filing buried in a distant part of another state. Use the information broker to determine if your subject has filed bankruptcy in *any* of the states to which your background investigation has led.

If you get a hit, the information broker will give you an extract that will contain all or most of the following information:

♦ CASE NUMBER

♦ DATE FILED

♦ PRIMARY DEBTOR NAME AND SOCIAL SECURITY NUMBER

♦ SECONDARY DEBTOR NAME AND SOCIAL SECURITY NUMBER

♦ AMOUNT DISCHARGED

With this information, you can then write to the bankruptcy court concerned and get the entire file quickly. In the *Resource List* at the end of the book you will find telephone numbers of the primary bankruptcy courts in the United States.

TAXES

Tax information is collected by both the Federal government via the Internal Revenue Service, and by many state governments. Let's look first at the type of tax information you can access *legally.*

We discussed earlier how some individuals use a corporate shell to conceal their assets or liabilities. Any search for assets or liabilities in the name of the individual turns up negative because everything is held in the company name.

Many slick individuals who cannot manage money pay their personal bills on time, but have a corporation that is late in paying bills or state taxes. If your investigation has revealed that the subject owns a corporation, you will want to ascertain if the corporation is in good standing with the taxation authorities in its state of incorporation.

All states will release this information. You need to send a letter to the State Revenue or Taxation Department asking if a particular corporation is in good standing. The department will respond with a yes or no. The next logical step would be to obtain a business credit report from an information broker to see how the subject corporation's accounts are paid. Business credit reports are available to anyone.

The second type of tax information is personal income tax data.

Before we get started, I must remind you that the following methods are *illegal*, although commonly used by investigators to obtain a subject's income tax return.

If you can obtain the state or Federal tax return of a previous year, you can go a long way in confirming a lot of the information you have been given. It is very easy to obtain a previous year's tax return from the Internal Revenue Service.

Go to any IRS office and obtain the form that allows you to request a previous year's tax return. To get the return from a previous year you will need the full name and Social Security Number of the subject, along with his or her address at the time the return was filed. A nominal fee will be charged.

The IRS will send you the return in a few weeks. Once again, in doing this you have committed a Federal crime, but it is done all the time. The same procedure can be used to obtain the state income tax return of the subject from the state Revenue or Taxation department. The addresses of all state taxation departments follow.

STATE TAX DEPARTMENTS

The following is a list of all state tax department offices. State taxation and revenue offices are responsible for administering each state's taxation laws. All state sales, income, corporate, and excise taxes will be processed through these offices. Most states will release data to the public on the current tax compliance of corporations. Other tax information is more restricted, unless, as in the case of income taxes, the taxes have gone unpaid and the state has taken legal action against an individual. These legal actions then become a matter of public record.

ALABAMA

Revenue Department
50 North Ripley Street
Montgomery, AL 36132

ARIZONA

Revenue Department
1600 West Monroe
Phoenix, AZ 85007

ARKANSAS

Finance and Administration
PO Box 1272
Little Rock, AR 72203

CALIFORNIA

Board of Equalization
Sales and Use Tax Department
Sacramento, CA 94279

COLORADO

Revenue Department
Taxpayers Services Office
1375 Sherman Street
Denver, CO 80261

CONNECTICUT

Department of Revenue
92 Farmington Ave
Hartford, CT 06106

DELAWARE

Finance Department
PO Box 8911
Wilmington, DE 19899

DISTRICT OF COLUMBIA

Finance and Revenue
441 4th Street NW
Washington, DC 20001

FLORIDA

Revenue Department
5050 West Tennessee Street
Tallahassee, FL 32399

GEORGIA

Sales and Use Tax Division
Taxpayers Services Unit
270 Washington Street SW
Atlanta, GA 30334

HAWAII

Bureau of Conveyances
PO Box 2867
Honolulu, HI 96803

IDAHO

Revenue Operations Division
Taxpayer Services
PO Box 36
Boise, ID 83722

ILLINOIS

Revenue Department
Taxpayer Services
101 West Jefferson Street
Springfield, IL 62794

INDIANA

Revenue Department
Taxpayer Services Center
101 North Senate Avenue
Indianapolis, IN 46204

IOWA

Revenue and Finance
Taxpayer Services
Hoover Bldg
Des Moines, IA 50319

KANSAS

Revenue Department—Taxation
915 SW Harrison
Topeka, KS 66612

KENTUCKY

Revenue Cabinet
Tax Compliance
PO Box 181
Frankfort, KY 40602

LOUISIANA

Revenue and Tax Department
PO Box 201
Baton Rouge, LA 70821

MAINE

Taxation Bureau
State House Station 24
Augusta, ME 04333

MARYLAND

Comptroller Division
Compliance Section
301 West Preston Street
Baltimore, MD 21201

MASSACHUSETTS

Revenue Department
100 Cambridge Street
Boston, MA 02204

MICHIGAN

Revenue Bureau
PO Box 15128
Lansing, MI 48109

MINNESOTA

Revenue Department
Ten River Park Plaza
St Paul, MN 55146

MISSISSIPPI

Revenue Bureau Tax Division
PO Box 22828
Jackson, MS 39225

MISSOURI

Revenue Department
PO Box 311
Jefferson City, MO 65105

MONTANA

Revenue Department
State Capitol
Helena, MT 59620

NEBRASKA

Revenue Department
PO Box 94818
Lincoln, NE 68509

NEVADA

Revenue Department
Capitol Complex
Carson City, NV 89710

NEW HAMPSHIRE

Revenue Department
State House
Concord, NH 03301

NEW JERSEY

Taxation Division
State House, Cn269
Trenton, NJ 08646

NEW MEXICO

Taxation and Revenue
PO Box 630
Santa Fe, NM 87503

NEW YORK

Taxation and Finance Dept.
W.A. Harriman Campus
Albany, NY 12227

NORTH CAROLINA

Revenue Department
PO Box 25000
Raleigh, NC 27640

NORTH DAKOTA

Tax Division
State Capitol
Bismarck, ND 58505

OHIO

Taxation Department
30 East Broad Street
Columbus, OH 43215

OKLAHOMA

Tax Commission
2501 North Lincoln Blvd
Oklahoma City, OK 73194

OREGON

Revenue Department
State Capitol
Salem, OR 97310

PENNSYLVANIA

Revenue Department
Dept 280905
Harrisburg, PA 17128

RHODE ISLAND

Taxation Division
One Capitol Hill
Providence, RI 02908

SOUTH CAROLINA

Revenue Department
PO Box 125
Columbia, SC 29214

SOUTH DAKOTA

Revenue Department
700 Governors Drive
Pierre, SD 57501

TENNESSEE

Revenue Department
500 Deaderick Street
Nashville, TN 37242

TEXAS

Controller of Public Accounts
LBJ Office Bldg
Austin, TX 78774

UTAH

Tax Commission
210 North 1950 West
Salt Lake City, UT 84134

VERMONT

Tax Department
109 State Street
Montpelier, VT 05609

VIRGINIA

Taxation Department
PO Box 1880
Richmond, VA 23282

WASHINGTON

Revenue Department
PO Box 47476
Olympia, WA 98504

WEST VIRGINIA

Tax Department
PO Box 2389
Charleston, WY 25330

WISCONSIN

Revenue Department
PO Box 8933
Madison, WI 53708

WYOMING

Revenue Department
122 West 25th Street
Cheyenne, WY 82002

13

Investigating Famous People

At the beginning of this book we examined several instances of individuals who were able to hurt others through manipulation and deceit. Having explored the various sources of information available to the investigator, let us now see how we could go about proving or disproving the allegations of these individuals.

Let's start with the movie actress who has made numerous allegations against her family and others who have allegedly abused her over the years. As with any investigation, we need to first confirm the base identifiers. If they are not confirmed, the investigation may very well dead-end for lack of an appropriate match of name and birthdate on records.

When investigating a celebrity, the first step is to absolutely confirm the **birthdate**. Many celebrities are vain, and attempt to muddle their birthdates by quoting numerous different years and months to disguise (usually lowering) their age.

The same is true for the celebrity's *legal name*. Most celebrities use a stage name in dealing with the public. A check for records under the stage name may yield no results. All legal documents such as driver's licenses, voter registrations, property tax records, etc., will be done under the legal name to protect their privacy.

In the case of noted entertainment figures, legal names and birthdates can often be confirmed via one of the directories published about movie stars and other famous people in the *Who's Who* series of guides. Consulting one of these reference books can be a shortcut to confirming the basic identifiers of a celebrity.

One example of this technique was used in the case of a noted star of a Saturday morning children's program who was very popular in the late 1980s and early 1990s. The star of this show also went on to make a number of movies that were also popular with children and very successful.

This man was arrested on a public indecency charge in Florida a few years later. His arrest was made under his legal name, and this would have remained a relatively private affair if a reporter had not done his homework and learned the stage name of this man. A few hours later, his arrest was national news. This incident illustrates the value of having the base identifiers confirmed when backgrounding a star. Celebrities are often arrested or sued under their true names, and the public remains ignorant because no diligent news sleuth linked the screen or stage name to the true name.

Once you have confirmed the celebrity's name and birthdate, attempt to locate the Social Security Number. This can be done by first getting a good solid address, and then performing a **national identifier search** through the credit bureaus.

The **true address** of a celebrity can be best found via property tax or voter registration records. We saw earlier that the addresses on these records must be an *actual* physical residence, and not a mail drop or agent address. Check the voter registration records first. If there is no voter registration, check property records.

One property records dodge used by celebrities is to have their private **production companies** own their property. Locating the name of an actor's production company is not difficult. You can consult state incorporation records for all corporations in the star's name, or a motion picture industry directory that lists production companies by name and owner. The objective is a search for all property ownership records under the celebrity's legal, stage, and production company names.

The final source of address information on a star comes from **civil court records.** If the star was divorced or married, or was sued, consult these records for a current or previous address. Many stars will permit their homes to appear in upscale architectural magazines, and this can yield a current address. Even maps that are sold on Hollywood street corners may contain a valid address. The point is, even if the address you obtain is old, when you run the national identifier sweep it will probably link the old address to the current address where the celebrity resides today. Once you have this information, your background investigation can really pick up speed.

You should now have the celebrity's real full name, birthdate, Social Security Number, and current and former addresses. You are in a position to develop information on the celebrity as you would any other person. Begin by ordering the **driving record** of the star from all previous states of residence. This information should be augmented with **vehicle registration information**.

When searching for vehicles or real property, perform a search in the name of the star's production company as well as his or her legal name. Make sure to do this search in all states where the star has lived, or has family.

If you are attempting to verify a specific allegation a star has made, as in the case of the female sitcom star, check for **police reports** or **arrest records** of those involved in the alleged incidents. This brings us to an often overlooked fact when backgrounding major public figures. Although the celebrity may have taken substantial steps to guard his or her privacy, *people who work for them*, or their *friends*, most likely have not. These people are readily accessible to the determined sleuth.

The sitcom star has alleged child abuse and other abuse over the years by members of her family. Develop base identifiers on these family members and then run a check for criminal records on *them*. Most police departments will provide a printout of all calls received to a specific address and the nature of the call. Run her address at the time of the incident to see if any calls were made to the police concerning the allegations.

In the case of the sitcom star, all of these record sources yielded no results and no hard information was found to back up the allegations. One fact that will become quite clear as you investigate celebrities is that much of what is told to the public is hot air designed to create a larger-than-life image. Publicity agents and managers will make statements to the media about the star's wealth or assets as a way of boosting their image. A detailed search will often reveal that the seven million dollar home the star supposedly owns is a rental and in reality a much more modest home is owned by the person.

A final note on researching celebrities. All public figures were ordinary people before they achieved a high profile. Their lives were usually conventional until they were discovered or "made it" and became the people we see in the media. The best way to unmask the truth behind public figures is to go back to that point in their lives when they were still ordinary, and then work both backward and forward.

14

Special Cases

There may be times when the individual you are investigating has special problems, such as unpaid child support, or a history of milking worker's compensation schemes for an income. You may also come across situations where the standard searches yield no information about an individual. The special sources and methods in this chapter may help.

UNPAID CHILD SUPPORT

The problem of unpaid child support is an acute one that grows in size every year. The increased rate of divorce makes this situation common today. Even when a court order has been obtained to collect child support, the absent parent can move out of state to frustrate enforcement procedures.

To combat this problem, the Federal government has taken a number of steps in association with the individual states. The first was that all states now attempt to obtain the Social Security Numbers of *both parents* on the birth of child, and this information is often placed on the child's birth certificate. As we have seen, the SSN is an invaluable link when searching for an individual, regardless of who is doing the searching.

The second part of the program is to have Federal files searched at various agencies to see if any delinquent parents are expecting money from the Federal government. The Internal Revenue Service will then intercept tax refunds due the delinquent parent and send them to the state where the child support was owed. If a delinquent parent was receiving money from a government-funded student loan program, the funds might be cut off. The Social Security Administration files would be consulted to develop a current address on the individual.

Once the delinquent parent is located in another state, expedited procedures are in place to initiate legal processes in that state to have wages or assets attached. To coordinate all of this, the Federal government set up regional offices of the Federal Office of Child Support Enforcement. The addresses of these follow. If your investigation reveals that the subject has unpaid child support, these offices can assist you in locating him or her.

CHILD SUPPORT ENFORCEMENT OFFICES

OCSE Regional Representative
50 United Nations Plaza
San Francisco, CA 94102

OCSE Regional Representative
1961 Stout Street
Denver, CO 80294

OCSE Regional Representative
101 Marietta Tower
Atlanta, GA 30323

OCSE Regional Representative
105 West Adams Street
Chicago, IL 60603

OCSE Regional Representative
John F. Kennedy Federal Bldg
Boston, MA 02203

OCSE Regional Representative
Federal Building
Kansas City, MO 64106

OCSE Regional Representative
Federal Building, #408
New York, NY 10278

OCSE Regional Representative
3535 Market Street
Philadelphia, PA 19101

OCSE Regional Representative
1200 Main Tower Building
Dallas, TX 75202

OCSE Regional Representative
2201 Sixth Avenue
Seattle, WA 98121

PASSPORT RECORDS

Another possible problem you may face is determining if an individual has a passport and with it might have left the country. Passport records are maintained by the Federal government, and passport applications are public record documents. The Department of State is the agency responsible for issuing passports. A passport application record will contain the following information:

- FULL NAME

- DATE OF BIRTH

- SOCIAL SECURITY NUMBER

- PLACE OF BIRTH

- PARENTS' NAMES AND BIRTHPLACES

- MAIDEN NAME OF MOTHER

- MAILING ADDRESS

- DRIVER LICENSE OR ID CARD NUMBER

- BIRTH CERTIFICATE INFORMATION

- DATE OF LAST PASSPORT OR RENEWAL

To obtain the passport records of an individual you will need a name and birthdate, and will make a Freedom of Information Act request of the passport office. Your request will be processed, but it will probably take six to ten weeks before you receive the information. Write to the following address to locate passport records:

Passport Services
Freedom of Information Act
U.S. Department of State
Washington, DC 20423

WORKER'S COMPENSATION FRAUD

Some states allow public access to worker's compensation records. These records will reveal if an individual has a previous or ongoing claim, the nature of the injury, the employer at time of injury, birthdate, full name, Social Security Number, and mailing address. Worker's compensation records can be very useful in verifying the employment background of an individual. If your subject has had contact with any of the listed states, a search of the worker's compensation files may well be worth doing.

To access worker's compensation files, all that is usually required is the name and Social Security Number. As before, always write to the agency concerned and ask for a current fee schedule and whether there is an official form that must be used to access the information.

OPEN WORKER COMPENSATION FILE STATES

ALASKA

Worker's Compensation Division
PO Box 25512
Juneau, AK 99802

ARKANSAS

Worker's Compensation
Commission
625 Marshall Street
Little Rock, AR 72201

CONNECTICUT

Worker's Compensation Division
1890 Dixwell Avenue
Hamden, CT 06514

ILLINOIS

Illinois Industrial Commission
100 West Randolph
Chicago, IL 60611

IOWA

Industrial Commissioner's Office
1000 East Grand Street
Des Moines, IA 50319

KANSAS

Division of Worker's Compensation
900 Jackson
Topeka, KS 66612

MAINE

Worker's Compensation
Commission
State House, Room 27
Augusta, ME 04333

MARYLAND

Worker's Compensation
Commission
6 North Liberty Street
Baltimore, MD 21201

NEW JERSEY

Division of Worker Compensation
State Office Building
Trenton, NJ 08625

OKLAHOMA

Worker's Compensation Court
1915 North Stiles
Oklahoma City, OK 73105

HUNTING AND FISHING LICENSES

Another obscure source of information is hunting and fishing license records. Just as with motor vehicle records, these are public in most states. The problem with using them is that, until very recently, they were not easily accessible. Very frequently, old license applications were kept in boxes in a dusty room at the state Fish and Game Department.

A new Federal program is now making these records very accessible, and hence more useful to the investigator. To track how birds migrate, the Federal Fish and Wildlife Service now requires states to obtain the full names and addresses of all persons obtaining hunting and fishing licenses. This computerized information is then passed on to the Federal government on an annual basis.

Once this program is up and running nationwide, by 1998, all states will have hunting and fishing license data available on computer. The states that currently have these records available are California, Missouri, South Dakota, and Maryland. The addresses of these states' wildlife departments appear below.

The second problem with using these records is that only a relatively small percentage of people hunt or fish. If your subject does neither, these records are of no utility. On the other hand, if your subject is an avid sportsman, this can be a highly productive place to search.

STATE COMPUTERIZED HUNTING AND FISHING LICENSE INFORMATION

CALIFORNIA

Department of Fish And Game
3211 S Street
Sacramento, CA 95816

MARYLAND

Department of Natural Resources
PO Box 1869
Annapolis, MD 21404

MISSOURI

Missouri State Water Patrol
PO Box 603
Jefferson City, MO 65102

SOUTH DAKOTA

Wildlife And Marine Resources
118 West Capitol Avenue
Pierre, SD 57501

FEDERAL GOVERNMENT EMPLOYEES

Another special opportunity applies if your subject is or was an employee of the Federal government. As with military personnel, certain personnel records of Federal civil servants are available to the public via a Freedom of Information Act request. Most federal employees give up certain aspects of their privacy. In most cases, the following information will be divulged to you about a current or former civil servant:

- ◆ FULL NAME

- ◆ WORK ADDRESS AND ORGANIZATION

- ◆ CIVIL SERVICE GRADE

- ◆ TITLE

- ◆ POSITION

You must direct your request to the **Freedom of Information Officer** of the agency where your subject works.

It is possible for an enterprising individual to earn good money by performing investigations or working as an information broker. In many states, depending on the types of cases undertaken, you will not need an investigator's license. We will examine a profession in investigations in the next chapter.

15

Making Money in Investigations

Locating people or information can be a lucrative primary business or a profitable sideline. The methods revealed in this book are the same ones used by many private investigators every day. Many of the daytime talk shows feature stories about how people were reunited with long-lost loved ones via a private investigator. The key to starting a people locator business is to first understand what activity requires a license and what does not.

LICENSING REQUIREMENTS

In most states, if you use the title of "investigator" or advertise "investigations" you *must* be licensed. Licensing may range from a mere formality in some states to a considerable expenditure of time and money in others. Investigators can use the title, conduct surveillance, and have access to certain databases that are unavailable to unlicensed individuals.

If, on the other hand, what you are primarily doing is confirming given facts about an individual, or merely finding a current address, most states will not require you to obtain any type of license. These businesses usually advertise as *people locator* or *tracer* services. As we have seen, almost all of this work can be done from a distance.

Who would use such a service? First, we have people searching for a lost loved one or relative. You might also have requests from landlords, banks, and individuals who are owed money, but who are unable to locate the person. These are all potentially lucrative clients. You are not involved in the actual collection of the debt (which requires a license), but simply in ascertaining the current location of the individual.

INFORMATION BROKERS

If you decide to go into this business, you will want to establish relationships with one or more information brokers and use the methods of this book efficiently. By this I mean using the least expensive source first, moving on to another only if that source fails to yield information. Consider a case where you need to find a Social Security Number.

You could go directly to an information broker service and have it run a national identifier search. This will yield results, but it might be an unnecessary expenditure. First, check voter registration, motor vehicle records, driver's license, and local tax records. You may well locate the subject's SSN here for just a few dollars.

The point is that you must develop your own skills in retrieving information from sources and you should only rely on information brokers when it is necessary or impossible to get the needed data any other way. When you price a search, it should reflect your cost of obtaining the record plus a fee for your time and other expenses. Advertisements can be run in local newspapers, the national tabloids, and in the classified sections of magazines for reasonable rates. You could also contact rental management companies and banks directly for referrals.

The bottom line is that information brokers succeed to the degree to which they become a resource to their clientele. Many of the requisite skills and information sources are explained here, but the professional probably will need much more, including subscriptions to specialized data bases and publications, plus the establishment of relationships that will expedite information processing.

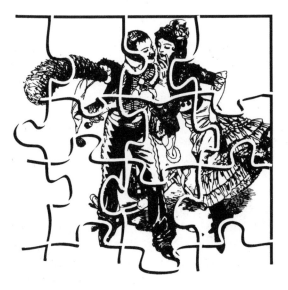

Pulling It All Together

You have learned how to obtain personal information from a variety of sources. As you develop your investigative skills, you may come across other information sources unique to your location.

The point of this is to notice that we have concentrated on information sources where most people will have records and the records are open for public inspection. To make your investigations effective, you need to follow a road map of sorts.

The first step in your investigation should always be to confirm or obtain the **base identifiers**. These normally will not change during the individual's lifetime. Only when these identifiers are confirmed can you then proceed confidently on the rest of your investigation. Base identifiers include the following:

- ◆ FULL NAME

- ◆ BIRTHDATE

- ◆ SOCIAL SECURITY NUMBER

- ◆ BIRTHPLACE

If you have an address, you can obtain an individual's Social Security Number and birthdate very quickly via a national identifier search through an information broker. But this information should always be confirmed with at least one public record. Remember that header information gets onto the credit report by way of the subject. If the subject is purposely attempting to alter or hide his or her name or Social Security Number, a header report will do little good on its own.

The next phase of investigation should involve obtaining a copy of the **subject's driving record** and **vehicle registrations**. If the driving record indicates citations or accidents, obtain a copy of the traffic citation or accident report from the relevant traffic court or state police agency. Examine the driving record carefully to see if it indicates that a license from a previous state was exchanged for a new one in the current state. If it was, obtain a copy of the driving record from the former residence state.

Between the credit bureau header report and the driving record, you should have a historical listing of addresses where the subject has lived. Now is the time to perform a **criminal record check**. If the subject has lived in a state where you can access the state crime repository, contact that agency. Otherwise, write to the court clerks in each county, as well as the adjacent counties, where the subject once lived.

At the same time, consult the three SSN charts in this book to determine if the **Social Security Number** used is valid, has actually been issued, and applies to someone who is the apparent age of the subject.

Next, check for local **civil judgments**, **property tax records**, and **voting records**. The information on these documents should serve to confirm what is contained on the driver record and statements made by the subject. Obtain a copy of the subject's **birth certificate**.

If the subject has indicated service in the **military**, order a copy of the service record. Confirm **degrees** directly with the colleges claimed.

The strategy should be clear. Go through the subject's life in reverse chronological order, obtaining the records of each stage of that life. Then put it all together. When you are finished, you should have a good idea of the type of person he or she is and what kind of life the subject has led. Only then will you be able to determine if this person should be a friend, an enemy, or a lover...

Appendix A:
Information Brokers

We earlier discussed how information brokers can be used to conduct a search to locate an individual. The search example we examined was the national identifier or address update search, which returns the Social Security Number of an individual when the only information available is the subject's name and last known address.

Information brokers can provide many services, and the price of these services has fallen dramatically over the last few years with the proliferation of computers. Many new companies have gotten involved in the information brokerage business, and this increased competition has forced a drop in prices. Many new information brokers will sell searches directly to the public. A purchaser need not be a private investigator or licensed collection agency to use them. Some brokers now have Internet sites which allow a client to perform a search right over the World Wide Web with their own computer and modem, charging to a credit card. We will examine Internet search providers in more detail in the next appendix.

If you are charging customers to perform searches, the same admonition about using brokers applies, even at the new lower prices. All information brokers are in business to make a profit, and the prices of their searches reflect this fact. Consider the following example:

You are attempting to locate an individual with whom a long lost friend wishes to reunite. Your customer has the full name and a former address. You could go directly to your information broker and run an address update search. This will likely yield you immediate results, but it may be relatively expensive.

If you appraise the situation with a little more care, you will see that this person can probably be located much more cheaply, and almost as quickly. This is not a skip trace or someone who has run out on their family and does not want to be found. This person is living openly, under his/her own name.

The place to begin this search is with a **national telephone database search**. In 90 percent of cases like this, you will score a hit and locate your individual. This search should cost you pennies, assuming you have purchased one of the excellent national telephone database programs available for about a hundred dollars, or used one available at the public library. A national telephone search can also be run at no charge, over the Internet. We will show how to do this in the next appendix.

The reason more companies are entering the information brokerage business is that more information sources are being computerized by their compilers, making the task less specialized. One example of such a newly available search is a **nationwide property analysis**.

This search goes far beyond simply telling you if someone owns property. It combines census bureau records with property tax records maintained by counties. If you know the address or telephone number of a particular piece of property you can glean the following information from this search:

- FULL NAME OF PROPERTY OWNER

- BIRTHDATE OF PROPERTY OWNER

- NAMES OF OTHER HOUSEHOLD MEMBERS

- APPROXIMATE VALUE OF PROPERTY

- DATE PURCHASED

- HOW LONG OCCUPIED BY CURRENT OWNER

- TYPE OF DWELLING

This search is available from a number of brokers, but is available most cheaply from a surprising source—the **Los Angeles County Public Library**. Believe it or not, this library has become one of the largest information brokers in the nation. It's at (213) 228-7000.

They offer a service called *FYI*—For Your Information. This service performs all of the functions of most information brokers—except they do it at a cut rate price. The fact that they are an arm of county government and deal in large volume with all major information providers allows them to undercut most competition. The only drawback is that they are not as quick in performing searches as are some of the commercial brokers. This is more than outweighed by the fact that they have direct access to all three major credit bureaus, many state motor vehicle departments, and have numerous proprietary databases. The other advantage to *FYI* is that these searches are available to the public, with no qualification required. Many information brokers will only sell pared down versions of their search to non-licensed individuals, or if they do sell the same searches to both types of customers, they will charge the individual requester more.

FYI can provide the following searches:

- HOUSEHOLD PROFILE

- ADDRESS UPDATE

- SOCIAL SECURITY SEARCH

- NATIONAL IDENTIFIER

- MOTOR VEHICLE REGISTRATIONS

- DRIVING LICENSE RECORDS

- REAL PROPERTY OWNERSHIP

- SOCIAL SECURITY DEATH INDEX SEARCH

- MISSING LINK SEARCH

- NATIONAL TELEPHONE INDEX SEARCH

- CUSTOMIZED SEARCHES

One of the most interesting searches the LA County Library can do is **missing link search**. The only input required for this search is a name and if known, a possible area of the country where the individual once lived. This area can be very broad—a state or region.

The missing link search will consult a number of different databases to develop information on the person. If the requestor has the age, or even an age range, say between twenty and thirty years old, the search becomes more precise. In most instances a missing link search will find the subject of the investigation. This search is not inexpensive, and it is not a search every information broker can provide because it requires access to multiple databases.

Before we look at the offerings from other companies, we need to give a few caveats to the buyer.

Information brokers compete with each other, and this competition leads to overstating certain capabilities and to overselling. One type of search where this frequently happens is searches based on credit bureau header information. These are the searches that perform address updates, locate unknown Social Security Numbers, and search the databases for a particular Social Security Number.

These searches are truly comprehensive only if at least two, and preferably all three major credit bureau databases are consulted. This is because a person's file at the credit bureau will reflect bureaus to which his creditors report. If your subject has creditors who report only to TRW, he or she will not have any records at the other two bureaus.

The second reason it is important to check more than one bureau is that the various credit bureaus are stronger in certain parts of the nation than in others. It is possible that if your subject has lived in only one geographic area his entire life, he will only have files at one bureau.

The only way to know for sure if an information broker pulls from all three (or at least two) sources on these searches, is to ask. If the broker gives you a bunch of double-talk, or says that it is a company secret, take your business elsewhere. All legitimate brokers will tell you from how many bureaus they pull header data.

Another potential problem can occur when an information broker not only provides header data, but also supplies complete credit reports to customers who go through the credit bureaus' screening procedures. When this is the case, header data reports to those clients without clearance for full credit reports are frequently truncated and not very useful.

This happens because the credit bureaus do not like to have their information sold to both grant credit and to locate deadbeats at the same location. If an information broker sells both types of reports, he frequently must remove information such as birthdates, telephone numbers, and employers from the header reports sold to the non-credit report client.

Another buyer warning is that you should select an information broker that has the coverage you actually need. Many brokers are very strong in their home state and surrounding states, but have scant coverage in other parts of the nation. If your needs are primarily within your own state, a local broker who is strong in your area may yield better results than a nationwide broker. Conversely, if you need a nationwide search, you should use a broker that has the broadest capability.

One area where information brokers have experienced tremendous growth is in **tenant screening** and in **pre-employment investigations**. A number of firms have sprung up to serve these specialized needs. One such company is **Avert**, which specializes in pre-hire background checks. Neither the publisher nor the authors are making a specific recommendation of this firm: they are used as an example of what's available out there.

The point here is to read sales brochures carefully, and do not be lulled into paying more for a search simply because the advertising makes it seem like you are getting more than there really is. This book has armed you with the necessary tools to make an informed judgment.

A company like Avert can be very useful because they can get *hardcopy records* for you if you want them. This can be very important. When you deal with an information broker, most of the time you will receive a record extract or recorded summary of the actual document. If you check for a vehicle registration, you will receive a summary of what is on that registration—not the actual vehicle registration itself. Most of the time this is acceptable. There may be occasions where you want to receive the actual hardcopy record. This might be of a court judgment, property title, or driving record. Corporations such as Avert can, for an added fee, have a local source go and obtain the hardcopy record for you.

Here's how to contact Avert for full details of the wide range of investigative services they offer:

> Phone
> *(800) 367-5933*
>
> Fax
> *(800) 237-4011*
>
> Modem
> *(800) 838-7722*
>
> Internet
> *http://www.avert.com*

The Registry is an information broker that specializes in providing tenant screening for landlords. In the section on records available at your local courthouse, we listed eviction orders and other rentals related orders courts can issue. Information brokers such as The Registry have compiled a nationwide database of such records, and made them accessible by name, birthdate, and Social Security Number.

Many landlords, in addition to running a traditional credit report, will also consult one of these databases. The reason for this is that many people with excellent credit are difficult tenants. They may frequently enter into disputes with landlords over one item or another, but they never let such arguments interfere with their credit rating. Or, they might have rented a house or apartment from a private party and been evicted, but the small landlord had no way to report this to the credit bureau. This database reduces the likelihood of renting to such people. You might also notice from The Registry's sales brochure that follows that they perform the same national fugitive check done by Avert.

Opening Doors for Property Managers

ill your community with residents who will pay the rent.

THE NUMBER ONE PREDICTOR OF WHETHER OR NOT AN APPLICANT WILL PAY THE RENT, the Registry Check provides property managers and real estate professionals with access to Landlord/Tenant Court records from across the nation. Each report scans The Registry's database for any cases of:

- Eviction
- Judgment for possession
- Judgment for possession and rent
- Property damage
- Failure-to-pay rent
- Unlawful detainers

enant Account Records:

Available with each Registry Check, Tenant Account Records provide the most immediate rental information available to the industry. Supplied by a national network of property managers who have rented or are currently renting to the applicant, Tenant Account Records or TARs are rental information on the applicant as reported by the property managers themselves. Property managers taking part in the TAR Program report move-ins, move-outs and any skips or evictions as soon as they happen. Tenant Account Records also allow the reporting of an excellent rental history that, at times, can be the only positive credit history an applicant may possess.

The Registry offers a full line of products and services designed to decrease rental risk for property managers. Resident screening including Landlord/Tenant Court records has proven to be the most effective means of choosing residents who will pay the rent.

Credit reports alone provide about 10% of the information needed to process an application. Credit bureaus report information such as: payment histories from creditors only and civil money judgments (no possession, property damage or case filings are reported). The Registry provides industry-specific rental histories plus all credit bureau information. Here are just a few of The Registry's other on-line services:

■ Credit reports from Trans Union, Experian (TRW) and Equifax

■ National Criminal Check

■ National Wanted Fugitive Check

■ Auto-Notify and Skip Trace

■ CreditGram

he First Step in Crime Prevention:

Crime prevention is an increasing concern for property managers across the United States. Protecting a community from drug trafficking, violence, theft, etc. is a large task for any neighborhood, especially a rental community. This is why The Registry provides access to national Criminal and Wanted Fugitive Checks - as a deterrent from major crime. The reputation of a community and safety of existing residents depend on informed rental decisions.

"I could not be happier with my decision to use The Registry. Just yesterday I ran a Registry Check and credit report. The individual's credit was perfect, however, he had been in tenancy court 4 times! I would recommend using The Registry to any apartment community that is interested in bringing in the best possible resident."

Rachel Rutman, Property Manager
Colony Oaks and Hidden Lake
North Brunswick, New Jersey

Time is valuable. The time it takes to process an application could mean the loss of a good resident. Time management is more than just the latest 'buzz word' in property management - this is why The Registry developed *RegAccess* software.

eports in Seconds!

The Registry's many products and services are accessible through a PC, credit prompter, fax or mail. For PC users (automated accounts), *RegAccess* software is available. *RegAccess* is The Registry's own, proprietary resident screening software. With *RegAccess* the resident selection process is made quick and easy with such features as:

> a Windows based format - run a Registry Check, credit report or order a Criminal Check at the click of the mouse!

> run reports in seconds! The ability to process the application while the applicant is still in the office or save the reports and print them later.

raining to Excellence:

The key to efficient, successful resident screening is proper training - from how to read reports to how to use the software. Upon membership with The Registry, property managers and their staff are provided with on-site training. As part of The Registry's continuing pursuit of excellence in proper screening, *Resident Screening Workshops* can be scheduled at the convenience of the management company.

Reference materials are available to members, such as '*The Survival Guide to Resident Screening*'. The Registry's Survival Guide walks through the application process from application, to credit report, to Registry Check. Using case studies, this manual tells how to read reports and apply each piece of the resident screening puzzle to get a complete picture of the applicant's rental background.

"Something as major as selecting a resident should never be considered a minor detail."

esident Retention and Collections:

The Registry offers services designed specifically to increase resident retention and collections such as *Auto-Notify* and *Skip Trace*.

<u>Auto-Notify</u> helps managers retain quality residents as well as keep track of those residents about to skip. Auto-Notify identifies residents who have applied for housing at other communities and notifies the property manager of their plan to leave. With this valuable tool, managers are given the opportunity to find out why a resident may want to leave and the chance to convince them to stay or apply for housing at a sister property. If the resident had plans of breaking their lease, managers are already aware before they skip and have a better chance of collecting rent due.

<u>Skip Trace</u> is a service that will locate a resident after they have skipped. Skip Trace helps property managers locate a resident who has 'skipped out' on their rental obligation and begin collecting overdue rent.

"When we first spoke to you in 1994, you promised us 'More information, faster, for less money.' Well we've seen that and more! There are other reasons we use The Registry, quality service, value, responsiveness, flexibility, training, commitment and personal attention. We appreciate that The Registry is continuing to provide the same quality of services at the same reasonable prices. The expanding list of services and regional coverage only enhance the value of membership with The Registry."

Denise Miller, Controller

P.M. Group, Inc.

Brighton, Michigan

To Profitability. . .

For more than a decade The Registry has been saving property managers tens of thousands of dollars in eviction and related costs. How? by providing them with rental histories on their applicants, information not found on the application or credit report!

"EVICTIONS ARE *PREVENTABLE* BECAUSE THEY ARE PREDICTABLE"

Managing risk through properly screening each application with Landlord/Tenant Court records will increase your bottom line. The savings in evictions costs (including filing fees, back rent, vacancy loss, refurbishing costs, etc.), property damage, legal fees and management time and stress could be the difference between a thriving community and one with low profits and high turnover.

"As the President and Chief Operating Officer of The Hamilton Company, I can attest to the usefulness and effectiveness of The Registry. We manage close to 3,000 residential units and run on average 2,500 credit checks a year. From this we have found that running just a credit check is not always sufficient or an efficient way of screening prospective tenants.

Using The Registry, we feel we've paid for the year's usage in just 6 months from saved evictions. We're not only saving money, we're saving time since we've installed The Registry's system in all of our satellite offices in order to expedite and streamline the approval/rejection procedure.

Our company highly recommends using The Registry."

Carl A. Valeri, President & COO
The Hamilton Company
Boston, Massachusetts

Applying consistent resident screening procedures will avoid Fair Housing violations. The creation and submission to a list of criteria set as standard procedure for the approval or rejection of a rental application should be a priority for all property managers.

By providing members with manuals such as 'The Survival Guide to Resident Screening' and training workshops, The Registry is helping property managers train staff members to read the reports and apply consistent criteria for screening the applications.

Make The Registry's products and services part of your company's criteria for the approval or denial of applications. The Registry takes pride in over a decade of helping property managers *Take the Risk Out of Renting.*

"Having the best tools is important, but tools alone will not make you a craftsman.
It also takes skill, and that means training and practice. This is especially true of the craft of evaluating applications consistently."

-Felicia Queen
Southern Management Corp.

"We thoroughly train our staff to use and cross-reference every aspect of the credit report, Registry Check, and the verification process. The result has been 10's of thousands of dollars in savings for delinquencies and turnover costs for skips and evictions. The cost of training is minor in comparison. As part of our training classes, our Registry Account Representative teaches a portion of our application processing and approval class. This not only saves our company time and money, but gives our staff the opportunity to ask very specific questions regarding the use of all of The Registry's services. This in-depth understanding has caused them to fully utilize all of the services that The Registry provides."

Felicia Queen, Director of Marketing
Southern Management Corporation

Registry Check
Landlord/Tenant Court records filed against your applicant. This detailed report includes any filings for failure-to-pay rent, evictions, judgments, possession and/or property damage cases filed against an individual. Know the rental history of your applicant before you rent to them!

Credit Reports

experían, formerly ***TRW***

Ⓜ *TRANS UNION*

EQUIFAX

National Criminal Check
Protect your community from becoming inhabited by dangerous criminals with Criminal Check, a nationwide, county-by-county criminal record search for conviction records existing for your applicant.

Wanted Fugitive Check
Ensure that you are not renting to fugitives fleeing from the law with the added protection of a Wanted Fugitive Check. Identify wanted fugitives applying for residence or employment in your community and breathe a little easier!

Tenant Account Records
FREE with the Registry Check. TARs (Tenant Account Records) are previous and/or ongoing lease performances supplied to The Registry by its nationwide network of landlords and property managers.

Auto-Notify
Automatic notification of potential skips BEFORE they leave. The Registry's Auto-Notify program alerts you when your current residents are out shopping for another apartment.

Skip Trace
Locate skip accounts for collection purposes with Skip Trace. Skip Trace tracks delinquent residents who have already relocated.

Risk Score
Converts all the information found on a credit report into a numeric score that summarizes an applicant's credit history.

★ ★ ★ ★

Take the Risk Out of Renting

COURT & CREDIT
INFORMATION SERVICES
The Registry Corporate Headquarters
11140 Rockville Pike, Suite 1200
Rockville, Maryland 20852
(800) 999-0350
FAX (301) 984-7312

Beware of information brokers that offer to provide records that would be **illegal for you to obtain** without a signed release from the subject. These include such privacy matters as credit reports, tax returns, birth certificates, medical records, and other restricted data. If you get caught obtaining a record to which you have no legal right, especially credit reports, you can face massive civil penalties and possible criminal prosecution. The best policy is to deal only with reputable firms, and not to request searches for information to which you have no legal right.

As stated repeatedly, some searches can be performed without the use of information brokers. This category includes employers (to whom simple phone calls can be made) and **credential verification**. As we have seen in the chapter on educational records, most universities, colleges, and even trade schools will verify graduation dates, programs of study, and academic honors via telephone or mail, almost always at no cost.

Don't spend money unnecessarily. Check the skill levels and geographic coverage of brokers, and choose one who ordinarily handles exactly the sort of request you're making. Demand a written estimate, or better—a firm commitment—of the cost of the data you need, and a schedule for getting it. Don't prepay except for a deposit.

Appendix B:
Online Searching
Resources and Techniques

The Internet offers a relatively new and highly effective set of methods to perform many of the searches described in this book. Online searching via the Internet offers many advantages, the main one being *anonymity*. No one knows who or what you are searching for, and you can view the results in the privacy and comfort of your own home.

The privacy aspect can be a big consideration if you are researching a public figure, politician, a prospective spouse, or even your boss. Many searches can be conducted over the Internet at cost-effective prices. These searches tend to be database searches that do not require someone to physically go pull a record. The good news is that many new sources of information are being converted to computerized form, and many information brokers are realizing that allowing customers to run their own searches via the Internet from home computers is more profitable than other forms of access. Once again, we must look at a number of different providers, and look carefully at what each offers via the Internet.

The first company to offer complete Internet searches was **NCI**, or **National Credit Information**. NCI is one of the first information brokers and has been in business for over a decade. NCI is affiliated with Datafax, an information broker that is part of the Thomas Investigative Publications Group.

NCI offers two modes of Internet access. One allows anyone at their web site to simply log in and run a search, paying online with a credit card. The other method is to become a member of NCI, and then run searches with a password. Before we go into details on the relative benefits of one access mode over another, we need to give directions to locate their website.

The best way to get to NCI is via the web site operated by *PI Magazine*, a publication of the Thomas Group:

```
http://www.pimall.com
```

Once you have loaded this site, you'll see hypertext directing you to numerous other sites or locations, both within this site and external to it. Click on the hypertext "Information Brokers". This will load a listing of such brokers onto your screen. Scroll down the list until you reach "NCI", and click.

NCI offers the following searches via the Internet:

- ♦ MULTISTATE VOTER REGISTRATION CHECK

- ♦ ADDRESS UPDATE SEARCH

- ◆ SOCIAL SECURITY NUMBER SEARCH

- ◆ UNKNOWN SOCIAL SECURITY NUMBER SEARCH

- ◆ SOCIAL SECURITY DEATH INDEX SEARCH

- ◆ DATE OF BIRTH SEARCH.

NCI offers reports to both members and nonmembers. The difference between the reports consists of the number of sources consulted and the amount of information downloaded from each such source. All of their currently available Internet searches are credit bureau header searches, with the exception of the death index search and voter registration check.

The nonmember search will only consult one of the credit bureaus, whereas the member search will frequently contain birthdate or birth years, home telephone numbers, or employer information. The decision to become a member is a personal one. It involves filling out a short form online, and providing your telephone number.

The other advantage NCI offers is true real-time turnaround on your searches. Most header searches are returned to you while you are still online—usually no more than a three minute wait. No other information broker offers this service to nonmember clients.

Another advantage of NCI is that their site is very easy to use for people who are not computer experts. When a report is run as a nonmember, a temporary Web address is created for you that will contain the report results. The information will be displayed at this address for ten days.

The most interesting new feature that NCI offers online is the multistate voter registration search. Until recently, voter registration records were not that handy as a search tool because access to them was manual only. Now the voter registration records of the following states have been compiled into a computer database:

- ◆ ALASKA

- ◆ ARKANSAS

- ◆ COLORADO

- ◆ CONNECTICUT

- ◆ DISTRICT OF COLUMBIA

- ◆ LOUISIANA

- ◆ MAINE

- ◆ MASSACHUSETTS

- ◆ MICHIGAN

- ◆ MISSISSIPPI

- ◆ MONTANA

- ◆ NEW HAMPSHIRE

- ◆ NEW JERSEY

- ◆ NEW YORK

- ◆ NORTH CAROLINA

- ◆ OHIO

- ◆ OKLAHOMA

- ◆ PENNSYLVANIA

- ◆ SOUTH CAROLINA

- ◆ SOUTH DAKOTA

- ◆ TEXAS

- ◆ UTAH

- ◆ WASHINGTON

- ◆ WEST VIRGINIA

- ◆ WISCONSIN

Voter registration searches can be valuable because they contain biographic information and *true* residential addresses of the subject. Even individuals who do not have a file at a credit bureau may well be listed in the voter registration records.

NCI's voter registration search allows you to search any or all of the states that are available on the database. The NCI search will return the first 100 records that match the input data that you provide. To use this search *effectively* requires further explanation.

Every state, and frequently, counties within the same state, use a different format to record voter registration information. Some states and counties record the full name, birthdate, Social Security Number, gender, and address; others just record the name, birthdate, and address. You can increase your chances of locating your subject on this search by having an idea of the state your subject is registered to vote, and what particular information that state records on its voter registration form.

The problem with this search is that if you fill out *all* of the information on the search request form, you can actually *decrease* your chances of scoring a match on your subject. If your search criteria include all of the above mentioned information but the state in which you run the search does not record the Social Security Number on voter registration documents, your search will return a miss. This is due to the fact that the computer will assume that a missing Social Security Number means that the record is not the same as the one being sought. The same situation applies to birthdate and sex. If these are very common, you might winnow the search further with an address. Name and address are on all voter registration records, and your chances of obtaining a match improves with these data.

NCI's death index search is a check of the Social Security Death File, and is available with either name or Social Security Number. They also offer an online postal address forwarding check. A computerized database of the postal change of address cards for individuals and for magazine subscribers is consulted in real-time.

On the next several pages are reproductions of some of NCI's sales information (the information is also available at their Website). Another nice NCI feature is that they will allow you to see a sample of the type of report you will receive before you start.

Address Identifier Update Search

Credit Headers - sometimes called **Address Identifier Update Search** are available from the National Credit Information Network. Consumer credit report databases are searched for identifying information only, no FCRA regulated data is returned on non-member searches. This search will allow you to verify current and previous addresses of an applicant, lost friend, lost relative or any subject you are trying to find.

Credit Header Records - Facts

- Lists any **current** and/or **previous addresses** associated with the entry criteria.
- Returns any **Aliases** that are listed as being connected with the entry criteria.
- Detects and Displays if the name and/or SSN is being used by more than one individual, and by whom.
- Informs you of the **Date** the address was last reported as having an association with the eentry criteria.
- Your **Credit Card** (**Visa**, **Mastercard**, or **American Express**) will be charged **$13.50**

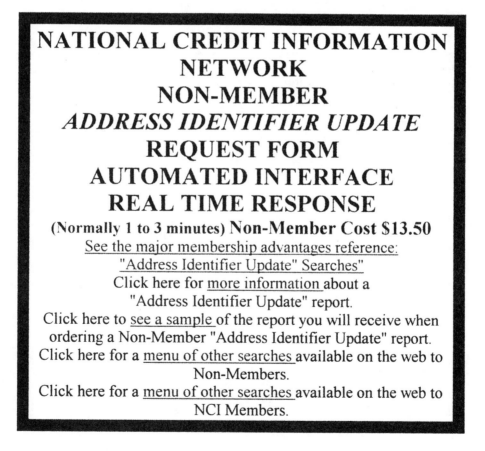

**NATIONAL CREDIT INFORMATION
NETWORK
NON-MEMBER
ADDRESS IDENTIFIER UPDATE
REQUEST FORM
AUTOMATED INTERFACE
REAL TIME RESPONSE**
(Normally 1 to 3 minutes) Non-Member Cost $13.50
See the major membership advantages reference:
"Address Identifier Update" Searches"
Click here for more information about a
"Address Identifier Update" report.
Click here to see a sample of the report you will receive when
ordering a Non-Member "Address Identifier Update" report.
Click here for a menu of other searches available on the web to
Non-Members.
Click here for a menu of other searches available on the web to
NCI Members.

```
REQUESTED      ... 9703040528
PROCESSED      ... 9703040601  (yymmddhhmm)
REQUEST CODE   ... Session # W3452819 / Request # 01



**  N A T I O N A L    C R E D I T    I N F O R M A T I O N    N E T W O R K  **
**      U N K N O W N    S O C I A L    S E C U R I T Y    #    S E A R C H      **
     REQUESTED ON Tuesday,  March 4th 1997 ... 06:01:20
     REQUEST CODE ... Session # W3452819 / Request # 01




[SUBJECT]                                    [SSN]         [BIRTH DATE]
LOOKINLAND, MIKE  P.                         553-88-8793   12/60
[ALSO KNOWN AS]                                            [TELEPHONE]
PLOOKINLAND,MICHAEL                                        486-2754




[CURRENT ADDRESS]                                          [DATE RPTD]
2839 E. 2960 S, SALT LAKE CITY UT. 84109                   3/96
[FORMER ADDRESS]
2036 HIGHLAND VIEW CI., SALT LAKE CITY UT. 84109           8/95
-----------------------------------------------------------------------
S P E C I A L    M E S S A G E S
 ***NCI FRAUD ALERT:FILE SSN ISSUED: 1967 - 1968; STATE: CA; (EST. AGE OBTAINED:

          06 TO 08)***
-----------------------------------------------------------------------
END OF REPORT
```

```
REQUESTED      ... 9703040626
PROCESSED      ... 9703040627   (yymmddhhmm)
REQUEST CODE ... Session # W3462629 / Request # 01



**  N A T I O N A L   C R E D I T   I N F O R M A T I O N   N E T W O R K  **
**      U N K N O W N   S O C I A L   S E C U R I T Y   #   S E A R C H      **
   REQUESTED ON Tuesday,  March 4th 1997 ... 06:27:09
   REQUEST CODE ... Session # W3462629 / Request # 01




[SUBJECT]                                    [SSN]        [BIRTH DATE]
BURTON, LEVAR  ROBERT                        565-13-9900  2/57
                                                          [TELEPHONE]
                                                          784-7550




[CURRENT ADDRESS]                                         [DATE RPTD]
5750 WILSHIRE BV., #580. LOS ANGELES CA. 90036            5/96
[FORMER ADDRESS]
15047 MARBLE DR., SHERMAN OAKS CA. 91403                  7/95
13601 VENTURA BV., #209. SHERMAN OAKS CA. 91423

--------------------------------------------------------------------
S P E C I A L   M E S S A G E S
 ***NCI FRAUD ALERT:INPUT CURRENT ADDRESS IS A MAIL RECEIVING/FORWARDING

         SERVICE
        :INPUT CURRENT ADDRESS HAS BEEN REPORTED MORE THAN ONCE
         (UNIT: 263,340,407,453,604,619)
        :FILE CURRENT ADDRESS REPORTED USED IN TRUE NAME FRAUD OR
         CREDIT FRAUD
        :FILE SSN ISSUED: 1972; STATE: CA; (EST. AGE OBTAINED: 14 TO
         15)
        :FILE ADDRESS, SSN, OR TELEPHONE NUMBER REPORTED BY MORE THAN
         ONE SOURCE***
--------------------------------------------------------------------
END OF REPORT
```

```
REQUESTED    ... 9703020517
PROCESSED    ... 9703020702   (yymmddhhmm)
REQUEST CODE ... Session # W3251756 / Request # 01



SCANNING ....... SOURCE #1 FOR ... 129-68-1658




* SOCIAL SECURITY NUMBER TRACE *                 129-68-1658

        NAME/SPOUSE                              SSN OWNER
        ADDRESS                                  ADDR RPT DATE


     1. LYRINTZIS, CONSTANTINOS S DR             SUBJECT
        550 BAYONA LP., CHULA VISTA CA. 91910    01/96
        4921 CAMPANILE DR., SAN DIEGO CA. 92115  12/95
        1820 E. DEL MAR BV., PASADENA CA.,205 91107
* L O O K *
***INPUT SSN USED IN DEATH BENEFITS CLAIM FOR CONSTANTIN

           LYRINTZIS.DOB:09/22/1960.DOC:08/15/1996
           :INPUT SSN ISSUED: 1985 - 1987; STATE: NY***
     2. LYRINTZIS, CONSTATIN S                   SUBJECT
        550 BAYONA LP., CHULA VISTA CA. 91910    05/96
* L O O K *
***INPUT SSN USED IN DEATH BENEFITS CLAIM FOR CONSTANTIN

           LYRINTZIS.DOB:09/22/1960.DOC:08/15/1996
           :INPUT SSN ISSUED: 1985 - 1987; STATE: NY***
     3. LYRINTZ, CONSTANTINOS S                  SUBJECT
        4921 CAMPANILE DR., SAN DIEGO CA. 92115  11/95
* L O O K *
***INPUT SSN USED IN DEATH BENEFITS CLAIM FOR CONSTANTIN

           LYRINTZIS.DOB:09/22/1960.DOC:08/15/1996

           :INPUT SSN ISSUED: 1985 - 1987; STATE: NY***
END OF REPORT



******   E N D   O F   N E T W O R K   T R A N S M I S S I O N   ******
```

BOOKMARK - THIS ADDRESS

This report can be later redisplayed by your browser at the following address for approximately 10 days

Before we examine other online information brokers' offerings, note that there are numerous sites on the Internet that will allow you to do *free* searches. You should never pay for a telephone number search because several companies offer this as a free service.

These companies have compiled a nationwide database of all telephone numbers in the United States. This is done by entering local telephone directory information into a central database. Some of these databases let you search by name, or to do a reverse search with either a telephone number or address.

It is recommended that an online search begin at one of these telephone number websites. If your search is intended to find someone with whom you've lost touch, as opposed to a skip trace, you may very well find them here because they are not hiding. Most people have listed telephone numbers, and are easily found. This can also be an excellent place to begin an investigation of an individual. These national telephone databases will return an address, and with an address you can then obtain the Social Security Number via a company such as NCI. An address will also allow you to obtain voter registration records, motor vehicle registrations, and a host of other information using the other methods outlined in this book.

The quality of national telephone record databases varies. Some of the companies maintain an ongoing updating process. Every time new listings are added, or old ones change, they enter the revised data into their file. The best companies are also careful to compile the phone listings everywhere in a given state, not just in larger cities.

This comprehensive coverage can make quite a difference, particularly in the western states, where many people still live in small towns. A telephone list compiler for Montana may include Billings, Bozeman, Butte, and Helena, the only cities of any size in Montana. But this will miss over *fifty percent* of that state's population. The best advice on using online telephone directories is to consult three or more before you give up on finding your subject.

Online telephone listings can be accessed by first going to:

```
http://www.yahoo.com
```

A screen will load offering a great variety of topics. You will want to click on "telephone numbers." You will then be offered a number of options for running telephone searches. Another way to locate different search possibilities is to simply click on "people locating" in the search engines Yahoo or Lycos. On Yahoo this will net you a page called the **United Internet Search Facility**. This page is a listing of many companies that allow free online searching, but it is by no means exhaustive. Two other telephone searches providers that are among my favorites are:

```
http://www.switchboard.com
```

```
http://www.whowhere.com
```

On the next page is a reproduction of the United Internet Search Facility page, and following that come sample pages from **Switchboard** and **WhoWhere.** These sites can also be used to locate businesses.

UNIFIED INTERNET SEARCH FACILITY

Telephone

Alaska Phone Directory / Locate people and business in Alaska.
American Yellow Pages / Lookup business telephone numbers.
AmeriCom Area Decoder / Lookup Area/City/Country Codes.
AT&T Toll-Free Directory / Lookup toll-free telephone numbers.
BigBook Yellow Pages / Lookup U.S. business phone numbers.
InfoSpace People Search / Search national white page directory.
GTE Super Pages / Lookup U.S. business telephone numbers.
Switchboard / Lookup business and private telephone numbers.
Yellow Pages Online / Lookup U.S. business telephone numbers.

UISFL|tm|: AtoZ: WebMaster: Notice:

Switchboard results   People | Business | Home

find a friend In Switchboard.people
the people and business directory

Listings 1 - 2   Modify Search | New Search

Bleecker, Amella Kailua Kona, HI 96740
Phone: (808)329-0079

Bleecker, David H 2440 Kuhio Ave, Honolulu, HI 96815-3347
Phone: (808)923-8149

                                              Add/Modify Your Listing

LookUp

Business

Services

Add & Update

WhoWhere? Home

WhoWhere? Features

E-mail Addresses

Instantly find e-mail addresses of friends, family and associates from the most comprehensive and popular directory on the Net. In addition, WhoWhere? offers unique value-added services to provide powerful searching and enhanced privacy features.

Phone Numbers & Addresses

A free directory assistance service that makes over 90 million US residential phone listings available at your fingertips.

WhoWhere? Communities

Find people based on past or current affiliations like school, interest groups, occupation, and more!

Personal Home Pages

The largest collection of categorized personal home pages of people from around the world. Explore, make friends, connect.

Internet Phone

A real-time directory, WhoWhere? Internet Phone provides point-and-click connectivity for users of standards compliant Internet phones such as Intel Internet Phone.

Companies Online

How often have you had this problem? You know the name of a company but you cannot find its web site even after wading through countless pages of search engine responses. Companies Online solves that problem. It is the most extensive worldwide directory of company whereabouts on the Net which includes company names along with their associated URLs, domain names, ticker symbols, and current stock prices.

WhoWhere? Edgar

Get free, convenient access to financial information and corporate performance for publicly held U.S. companies based on SEC Edgar filings. Use the powerful features of this personal research tool to track your investment portfolio.

U.S. Toll Free Numbers

Directory of U.S. Toll Free 800 and 888 numbers with over 300,000 current business listings.

Yellow Pages

Another online information broker is **Docusearch,** which performs all types of searches and will do searches for any category of client. They are a full service information broker. They make no bones about the fact that you can use their services to learn the secrets of those around you. This is a refreshing attitude from an information broker. Many brokers pretend not to cater to a lot of people who simply want to know their neighbor's business.

Docusearch does not offer the true interactive online searches that NCI does, but they come close, and they have other features that outweigh that disadvantage. You submit searches to Docusearch online via the Web. They will return your search results to your e-mail address, and many searches are returned within one day. Docusearch's Web address is:

> `http://www.docusearch.com`

They can also be reached via the PImall Web site, discussed earlier. One advantage Docusearch offers over NCI is that this company provides full search information to all clients. There is no need to become a member to have access to unedited search results. Their prices are higher, but still very competitive when you consider the fact that their searches are more comprehensive.

Docusearch offers the following searches:

- ◆ SOCIAL SECURITY TRACE
- ◆ ADDRESS UPDATE SEARCH
- ◆ UNKNOWN SOCIAL SECURITY NUMBER SEARCH
- ◆ CRIMINAL RECORD—STATE
- ◆ CRIMINAL RECORD—FEDERAL
- ◆ DRIVER RECORD SEARCH
- ◆ LICENSE PLATE SEARCH
- ◆ VEHICLE NAME SEARCH
- ◆ REAL ESTATE AND PROPERTY RECORDS
- ◆ LIENS AND CIVIL JUDGMENTS
- ◆ SURNAME SEARCHES
- ◆ BACKGROUND REPORTS

Docusearch also bundles many of their searches together and offers them at a value price. Their searches range from $9.00 to the most expensive at $99.00. As an example, let's compare the Social Security search offered by Docusearch to the nonmember search offered by NCI.

The NCI search for nonmembers will consult only one source, and in most cases will not return a birthdate or other personal identifiers. This search costs $16.00.

Docusearch will do an SSN trace on one source for $12.00, and they will return all of the information that appears on the search. The big difference comes with their package deal. For $44.00 they will search all three major credit bureaus, effectively giving you a search of the third credit bureau network free.

The same is true for their address update search. One source is $ 12.00, but all three are only $24.00. All of these searches are offered without the hassle of becoming a member.

Docusearch also offers tailored searches for specific needs. Two of these are the "Personal Dossier" and the "Businessman's Dossier." These are both background type searches that examine a myriad of databases for criminal records, bankruptcies, civil judgments, and other information. Docusearch is like having an electronic private investigator available. The next five pages reproduce Docusearch information available on the Internet.

To: ipgbooks@indexbooks.com
Reply-To: respond@docusearch.com
Date: Fri, 16 May 97 06:01 EDT
From: Docusearch Autoresponder <respond@docusearch.com>
Subject: Automated Reply!

This is a text version of our web site. To place an order, please go to:
http://docusearch.com   or write us at: info@docusearch.com

WELCOME TO DOCUSEARCH

"We find people and information about them"

Now any Internet-savvy individual can locate lost friends, track down
debtors and deadbeats, or discover the secrets of the people with whom
you associate. It's all totally professional, completely legal, and
entirely confidential.
Taking years of experience from highly paid private investigators and
surveillance experts, DocuSearch has come to bring resources
(previously available only to big business and the wealthy) to you!
DocuSearch offers an array of informative searches designed to help you
find the information you need to know, today! No matter where you live
in this world; you can now access data about people residing in the
United States. This is the information age, and information is power!
Controversial? Maybe; but wouldn't you sleep easier knowing a little
bit more about a prospective business partner, employee, baby-sitter,
neighbor or significant other? All search requests are ordered here, on
our Secure Server and the results are returned by e-mail so you can view
them in the comfort and privacy of your home or office. All information
obtained will be held in the strictest of confidence. Today begins a new
era in the information age: the age of personal data searches conducted
on private individuals by private individuals using the power and speed
of the global networks.

SEARCH DESCRIPTIONS

LOCATE DOSSIER

This dossier consists of three separate searches, all for the purpose of
locating a persons current and previous address. They are: Social Security
Number Search, Telephone Number Search, and Bankruptcy Search. You can
check out these searches on their respective pages.

This special search package costs only $29.00 and is available in all States.

Approximate return time: 1 day.

Required information for this search: Subjects's full name, previous known
address and telephone number.

PERSONAL DOSSIER

Someone new in your life? Are you about to take in a new roommate to share

This search costs $29.00 and is available in all states.

Approximate return time: 2-4 days.

Required information to perform this search: subject's full name, county and State {where search is to be performed}. Date of birth and social security number are helpful. Note: only one county per search.

CIVIL RECORDS

Want to know about pending or previous civil litigation? Does a prospective partner have a history of being sued?

CIVIL RECORDS- UPPER LEVEL

This search checks upper level court based on the county submitted. It provides information consisting of upper level civil filings. Each county varies in regard to what is maintained at its upper and lower courts depending on the dollar amount involved. Response may include plaintiff, defendant, case number, file date, cause of action and disposition or current status. Divorces, domestic or family law, child support (reciprocal) actions, name changes and probate may or may not be included, depending on the court. It may also include law firms involved with the case. This search covers the past seven years. The final report will indicate the dates searched.

If multiple records are found, DocuSearch will return detailed information on the three most recent cases and index information on any additional cases.

This search costs $29.00 and is available in all States.

Approximate return time: 2-4 days

Required information to perform this search: Subject's full name, county and state, where the search is to be performed. Helpful: Subject's date of birth and social security number.

CIVIL RECORDS-LOWER LEVEL

This search checks lower level court based on the city and county submitted. It provides information consisting of lower level civil filings. Each county varies in regard to what is maintained at its upper and lower courts depending on the dollar amount involved. Response may include cause of action, disposition or current status. It may also include law firms involved with the case. This search covers the past seven years. The final report will indicate the dates searched.

If multiple records are found, DocuSearch will return detailed information on the three most recent cases and index information on any additional cases.

To: ipgbooks@indexbooks.com
Reply-To: respond@docusearch.com
Date: Fri, 16 May 97 06:01 EDT
From: Docusearch Autoresponder <respond@docusearch.com>
Subject: Automated Reply!

state, where the search is to be performed. Helpful: Subject's date of
birth and social security number.

CIVIL RECORDS-UPPER & LOWER LEVEL

This search checks both upper and lower level courts based on the city and
county submitted. It provides information consisting of upper and lower
level civil filings. Each county varies in regard to what is maintained at
its upper and lower courts depending on the dollar amount involved.
Response may include cause of action, disposition or current status and
should include divorces, domestic or family law, child support actions,
name changes and probate. It may also include law firms involved with the
case. This search covers the past seven years. The final report will
indicate the dates searched.

If multiple records are found, DocuSearch will return detailed information
on the three most recent cases and index information on any additional cases.

This search costs $58.00 and is available in all States.

Approximate return time: 2-4 days

Required information for this search: Subject's full name, city, county and
state, where the search is to be performed. Helpful: Subject's date of
birth and social security number

DRIVERS & VEHICLE SEARCHES

DRIVING RECORD SEARCHES

An integral part of any background work, a driving record may provide
identifying information and insight into a person's character. Driving
habits such as speeding and reckless driving may be utilized in such a
determination. Information returned may include driver's license number,
class and status, full name, date of birth, physical description, dates of
convictions, violations and accidents, sections viloated, docket numbers,
court locations and accident report numbers.

This search costs $29.00 and is available in all states.

Approximate return time: 2-4 days.

Required information to perform this search: subject's full name, date of
birth, the state where the search is to be performed, and the subject's
driver's license number exactly as it appears on their license (the license
number is not required in the following states: CA, CO, FL, IL, IN,
ME, MI, MN, MT, NH, NM, NY, NC, OH, VA, WA, and WI).

LICENSE PLATE RECORDS

Want to know who is parked in your assigned spot? Someone hit your vehicle, then fled the scene?

Information from this search determines the ownership of the vehicle and all addresses assigned to that plate number and its VIN (vehicle identification number) in a particular state.

This search costs $30.00 and is available in all states except: GA, HI, and VA.

Approximate return time: varies from 2 days to 6 weeks, depending on the state in which the search is to be performed; most searches will take about one week.

Required information to perform this search: subject's license plate number and the state where the plate was issued.

VEHICLE NAME REGISTRATION

If you do not know a subject's license plate number or VIN (vehicle identification number), you can provide just their name, last known address, date of birth and/or Social Security Number. From this information, we can provide you with a list of all vehicles registered to that subject in a particular state.

This search costs $59.00 and is available in all states except for GA, HI, and VA.

Approximate return time: 2 days.

Required information to perform this search: subject's full name, last known address (street, city, state, and ZIP code).

FINANCIAL SEARCHES

REAL ESTATE AND PROPERTY RECORDS [CURRENT OWNER]

The Property search is useful for determining owners of a specific property. This search often return owners' names, parcel numbers, mailing addresses, property addresses, sale dates and amounts, land and inprovement values and exemptions.

This search costs $15.00 and is available in all states.

Approximate return time: 1 Days

Required information to perform this search: property's street address, city and state.

results obtained.

Q.) DO YOU PROVIDE ANY OTHER TYPES OF SEARCHES OTHER THAN THE ONES DESCRIBED ON YOUR PAGE?

A.) Yes. We provide many different searches. Some are not listed because they are restricted to
a small number of States. If there is a search you would like us to perform, please send us the
details and the State and we will return you a quote and the availability.

PAYMENT OPTIONS:

ALL CREDIT CARD TRANSACTIONS ARE VIA OUR SECURE SERVER

You may use any of the credit cards below :

VISA
MASTERCARD
AMERICAN EXPRESS
DISCOVER

For Your Added Protection: The customers address must match the credit card BILLING ADDRESS, or your order will NOT be processed.

You may also pay by cashiers check, money order or personal check. Simply send your order
form with the required information along with the cashiers check, money order or personal check
to:
DOCUSEARCH(sm)
7040 W. Palmetto Park Rd.
Suite 507
Boca Raton, Fl., 33433
Note to Personal Check Orders: All search results will be held until personal check
clears our bank.

Note: all prices listed are in U.S. funds.

TO PLACE AN ORDER, PLEASE GO TO OUR WEB SITE: HTTP://DOCUSEARCH.COM

FOR QUESTIONS, WRITE: INFO@DOCUSEARCH.COM

Another company that provides search services on the Web is **American Locator Service**. This company advertises heavily on daytime talk shows. They offer a unique proposition for the client. If they cannot locate the individual you are seeking they do not charge you a fee. Their locator search costs $47.50. This search consults databases from credit bureaus, telephone companies, mail order houses, and change of address records. They attempt to locate an individual whose name and other identifiers match those provided by the customer. My opinion of this search is that it should only be used if you have little or no information.

Consider the fact that if you have the name and previous address of an individual, an address update, or unknown Social Security Number, Docusearch will return the current address, SSN, telephone number, and birthdate, especially if you run this search through all three sources at Docusearch. Even the one source search at NCI will yield better results than the American Locator Search that does *not* give you any identifiers. The other firms will. If you do not have an old address, consult one of the online telephone directories first. This may give you a current address. Locating an old address might be possible via a voter registration check through NCI, and from there you can learn the SSN. The American Locator literature follows.

AMERICAN LOCATOR
a service of
SHEAFFER & ASSOCIATES

FIND ANYBODY, ANYWHERE NOW!

AMERICAN LOCATOR will help you find lost loves, former spouses, runaway spouses, parents/children lost through adoption; or anyone you have been unable to locate. **ALMOST EVERYONE HAS SOMEONE THEY WOULD LOVE TO HEAR FROM, BUT THEY HAVE NO IDEA HOW TO GET IN TOUCH WITH THEM.**

WE ARE THE PREMIER LOCATOR SERVICE IN THE UNITED STATES; AND WE KNOW HOW TO HELP YOU FIND YOUR MISSING PERSON!

We search data compiled by phone companies, credit bureaus, major mail-houses and many others.

OUR SERVICE IS GUARANTEED! If we are unable to match the information you give us, there is **ABSOLUTELY NO CHARGE TO YOU.** No other service we know of offers this guarantee. **WE CHARGE JUST ONE FEE WHEN WE FIND A MATCH FOR YOUR MISSING PERSON -**

$47.50

Have questions about how our sevice works? See "Freqently Asked Questions Page" below or link to one of the order pages and START YOUR SEARCH NOW!!

ORDER ON-LINE USING A CREDIT CARD

ORDER BY PHONE USING A CREDIT CARD

ORDER BY CHECK OR MONEY ORDER

ORDERING INSTRUCTIONS FOR USERS OF AMERICA ONLINE AND OTHER ISP'S OR BROWSERS WHICH DO NOT SUPPORT FORMS TRANSFER

FREQUENTLY ASKED QUESTIONS

Send an E-mail: SHEAFFER & ASSOCIATES

Page created by: SHEAFFER & ASSOCIATES
A Meadows Services, Inc. Company
P.O. Box 4104
Reading, PA 19606
Changes last made on: Wed *07 Feb 1997 13:10*

AMERICAN LOCATOR
a service of
SHEAFFER & ASSOCIATES

FREQUENTLY ASKED QUESTIONS

Q. Who is SHEAFFER & ASSOCIATES?

A. SHEAFFER & ASSOCIATES is a company formed by Credit and Collection professionals. We have decades of experience in locating people intentionally hiding from their creditors. Now we are doing something to help you find the person you are looking for. SHEAFFER & ASSOCIATES is A Meadows Services, Inc. Company.

Q. How does the AMERICAN LOCATOR SERVICE work?

A. We take the information you provide on the Credit Card Order form or the Check order form and compare it to data compiled by one or more of the following: Credit Bureaus, DMV's, Phone Companies, Major Mailhouses and many others. We will send you a list of up to 25 people that most closely match the information you provide. Please see our terms for details.

Q. I don't have much information on the person for whom I am searching, can you still help?

A. Absolutely. We have found matches to countless inquiries with just a first and last name. But remember, the more accurate, complete and recent the information you give us, the better our chances of finding an exact match to the person you are searching for.

Q. What should I expect to receive for my money?

A. You will receive by e-mail (or U.S. Mail if you don't have an e-mail account) a list of up to 25 names, addresses and telephone numbers (if published) for the people that most closely match the data you provide.

Q. Why should I use AMERICAN LOCATOR instead of another service?

A. There is only one fee $47.50; one of the lowest in the business. There are no hidden processing charges or other fees. The service is guaranteed; if we can't find a match to the data you provide, there is NO COST to you.

Q. Why is your service different from others I've seen on the 'Net?

A. There is no way we know of to search Credit Bureau, DMV and Mailhouse information on the 'Net. The other services like ours charge different rates for different searches, we charge just one fee if we find a match to the information you provide.

Q. I'm trying to place an order, but I keep getting error messages.

A. Unfortuanately not all ISPs (Internet Service Providers [Notably America Online]) and not all browsers support a function called "forms transfer". Please choose the appropriate ordering option if you are having problems with the others. Sorry for the inconvenience.

If you have further questions send us an E-mail: SHEAFFER & ASSOCIATES

Page created by: SHEAFFER & ASSOCIATES
A Meadows Services, Inc. Company
P.O. Box 4104
Reading, PA 19606
Changes last made on: Wed *07 Feb 1997 13:20*

Dig Dirt Inc. is another search firm available online that can be reached through PImall. Once again, the only problem is that only certain searches are offered to the public, and often at a relatively higher price. Some information brokers maintain this policy of only offering certain searches to the public because it maintains a continued veil of secrecy and mystery about the information they sell. After all, if every John Doe can access the same so-called confidential information online that a private detective or a policeman can, maybe it isn't actually so secret and the prices need to come down. That is exactly what is happening.

This book has illustrated that, for the most part, the only sources these companies and private detectives have are public record searches. What these groups previously had that the public did not, was access to these sources in a timely fashion. Now that barrier is falling away.

Other databases are becoming available online at a rapid pace. Essentially, any list that is now printed on paper can be computerized and made available online. For example, one consumer advocacy group publishes a listing of about ten thousand physicians in the United States who have either had their licenses to practice medicine revoked, face serious disciplinary action from state medical boards, or have been arrested for drug or alcohol abuse, or for other serious crimes. This listing is computerized and a doctor's status can be checked online by simply typing in his or her name and seeing if a match occurs.

Online searching relies on the same techniques as other searches described in this book. The more accurate your search information, the better will be the results you receive from these firms. Always have the full name spelled correctly, and have the correct values for any other personal identifiers that you know. Use the information that you do know to narrow the scope of your search, and try free or no cost databases first before you pay an online broker to run a search.

NOTE:

The nature of the Internet supports highly fluid "virtual companies," and even well-established information brokerages will frequently change their WWW sites, location information, capabilities, prices, accessibility, and limitations. This information, therefore, is provided as a guide, and is current as of mid-1997. The reader is encouraged to use search engines to locate other information sources, to validate locations/URLs of information brokers, etc.

Resource List

AIR FORCE PERSONNEL LOCATOR

To locate anyone in the Air Force.

(210) 652-5774; (210) 652-1110

AMERICAN BAR ASSOCIATION

Their Discipline Database tracks disciplinary actions against attorneys. They will also tell you whether or not an attorney's law school is accredited.

(312) 988-5000

ARMY PERSONNEL LOCATOR SERVICE

To locate anyone in the Army.

(317) 542-4211

AUTOMATED NAME INDEX

This firm provides credit histories, lawsuit information, criminal histories, corporate records, and other public and private records.

(818) 637-8625

AVERT, INC.

This company provides pre-employment investigative reports covering driving records, criminal verification of education records, etc.

(800) 367-5933

BANKRUPTCY COURTS

Bankruptcy filings can provide detailed information on the financial status and history of both individuals and companies. This information can actually be obtained with a touch tone telephone for those courts that provide a voice case information systems (abbreviated *vcis* in the listing below).

Alabama Northern District		
Northeastern Division		*(205) 353-2817*
Southern Division		*(205) 731-1614*
Eastern Division		*(205) 237-5631*
Western Division		*(205) 752-0426*
Alabama, Middle District		*(205) 223-7348*
Alabama, Southern District	**(vcis)**	*(205) 441-5638*
Alaska	**(vcis)**	*(907) 271-2168*
Arizona		*(907) 271-2658*
Phoenix Division		*(602) 640-5800*
Tucson Division		*(602) 670-6304*
Yuma Division		*(602) 783-2288*
Arkansas, Eastern District	**(vcis)**	*(501) 324-5770*
Arkansas, Western District	**(vcis)**	*(501) 324-5770*
California, Northern District:		
San Jose Division		*(408) 291-7286*
San Francisco Division		*(415) 705-3200*
Oakland Division		*(510) 273-7212*
Santa Rosa Division		*(707) 525-8539*
California, Eastern District	**(vcis)**	*(800) 736-0158*
	(vcis)	*(916) 551-2989*
California, Central District		
Los Angeles Division		*(213) 894-3118*
Santa Ana Division	**(vcis)**	*(714) 836-2278*
Santa Barbara Division	**(vcis)**	*(805) 899-7755*
San Bernardino Division	**(vcis)**	*(909) 383-5552*
California, Southern District		
San Diego Division	**(vcis)**	*(619) 557-6521*
Colorado	**(vcis)**	*(303) 844-0267*
Connecticut	**(vcis)**	*(203) 340-3345*
	(vcis)	*(800) 800-5113*
Delaware		*(302) 573-6174*
District of Columbia	**(vcis)**	*(202) 273-0048*
Florida, Northern District		
Pensacola Division		*(904) 435-8475*
Tallahassee Division		*(904) 942-8933*
Florida, Middle District		
Jacksonville Division		*(904) 232-2853*
Orlando Division		*(407) 648-6364*
Tampa Division		*(813) 225-7064*
Florida, Southern District		*(800) 473-0226*
		(305) 536-5979

Georgia, Northern District		
Atlanta Division		*(404) 331-5411*
Gainesville Division	**(vcis)**	*(404) 730-2866*
Newnan Division	**(vcis)**	*(404) 730-2866*
Georgia, Middle District	**(vcis)**	*(912) 752-8183*
Georgia, Southern District		
Savannah Division		*(912) 652-4100*
Hawaii		*(808) 541-1791*
Idaho	**(vcis)**	*(208) 334-9386*
Illinois, Northern District		
Chicago Division	**(vcis)**	*(312) 435-5670*
Rockford Division	**(vcis)**	*(815) 987-4350*
Illinois, Central District	**(vcis)**	*(217) 492-4550*
	(vcis)	*(800) 827-9005*
Illinois, Southern District	**(vcis)**	*(618) 482-9365*
	(vcis)	*(800) 726-5622*
Indiana, Northern District	**(vcis)**	*(219) 236-8814*
Indiana, Southern District		
Evansville Division		*(812) 465-6440*
Indianapolis Division		*(317) 226-6710*
New Albany Division		*(812) 948-5254*
Iowa, Northern District	**(vcis)**	*(319) 362-9906*
Iowa, Southern District	**(vcis)**	*(515) 284-6230*
Kansas	**(vcis)**	*(800) 827-9028*
	(vcis)	*(316) 269-6668*
Kentucky, Eastern District	**(vcis)**	*(800) 998-2650*
	(vcis)	*(606) 233-2657*
Kentucky, Western District	**(vcis)**	*(502) 625-7391*
Louisiana, Eastern District	**(vcis)**	*(504) 589-3951*
Louisiana, Middle District	**(vcis)**	*(504) 382-2175*
Louisiana, Western District	**(vcis)**	*(800) 326-4026*
	(vcis)	*(318) 676-4235*
Maine	**(vcis)**	*(207) 780-3755*
Maryland	**(vcis)**	*(410) 962-0733*
Massachusetts	**(vcis)**	*(617) 565-6025*
Michigan, Eastern District	**(vcis)**	*(313) 961-4940*
(includes Detroit)		
Michigan, Western District	**(vcis)**	*(616) 456-2075*
Minnesota	**(vcis)**	*(800) 959-9002*
	(vcis)	*(612) 290-4070*
Mississippi, Northern District	**(vcis)**	*(601) 369-8147*
Mississippi, Southern District		*(601) 965-5301*
Missouri, Eastern District	**(vcis)**	*(314) 425-4054*
(includes St. Louis)		
Missouri, Western District	**(vcis)**	*(816) 842-7985*
Montana	**(vcis)**	*(406) 496-3335*
Nebraska	**(vcis)**	*(800) 829-0112*
	(vcis)	*(402) 221-3757*

Nevada, Las Vegas Division		*(702) 388-6633*
Reno Division		*(702) 784-5515*
New Hampshire	**(vcis)**	*(603) 666-7424*
New Jersey	**(vcis)**	*(201) 645-6044*
New Mexico		*(505) 766-2051*
New York, Northern District	**(vcis)**	*(800) 206-1952*
New York, Southern District		
New York City Division		*(212) 682-6117*
White Plains Division		*(917) 682-6117*
New York, Eastern District	**(vcis)**	*(718) 852-5726*
New York, Western Division	**(vcis)**	*(800) 776-9578*
		(716) 846-5311
North Carolina, Eastern District		
Raleigh Division		*(919) 856-4418*
Burlingham Division		*(919) 237-0248*
North Carolina, Middle District	**(vcis)**	*(919) 333-5532*
North Carolina, Western District	**(vcis)**	*(704) 344-6311*
North Dakota		*(701) 239-5641*
Ohio, Northern District	**(vcis)**	*(216) 489-4731*
	(vcis)	*(216) 489-4771*
Ohio, Southern District		
Columbus Division	**(vcis)**	*(513) 225-2562*
Dayton Division		*(513) 225-2544*
Oklahoma, Northern District	**(vcis)**	*(918) 581-7181*
Oklahoma, Eastern District	**(vcis)**	*(918) 756-8617*
Oklahoma, Western District	**(vcis)**	*(405) 231-4768*
Oregon	**(vcis)**	*(800) 726-2227*
	(vcis)	*(503) 326-2249*
Pennsylvania, Eastern District	**(vcis)**	*(215) 597-2244*
Pennsylvania, Middle District		*(717) 782-2260*
Harrisburg Division		
Wilkes-Barre Division		*(717) 826-6450*
Pennsylvania, Western District	**(vcis)**	*(412)-355-3210*
Rhode Island	**(vcis)**	*(401) 528-4476*
South Carolina	**(vcis)**	*(800) 669-8767*
	(vcis)	*(605) 330-4459*
Tennessee, Eastern District	**(vcis)**	*(800) 767-1512*
	(vcis)	*(615) 752-5272*
Tennessee, Middle District		*(615) 736-5584*
Tennessee, Western District	**(vcis)**	*(901) 544-4325*
Texas, Northern District		
Amarillo Division		*(806) 376-2302*
Dallas Division	**(vcis)**	*(214) 767-8092*
Fort Worth Division		*(817) 334-3802*
Lubbock Division		*(806) 743-7336*
Texas, Southern District		
Corpus Christi Division		*(502) 888-3484*
Houston Division	**(vcis)**	*(800) 745-4459*
	(vcis)	*(713) 250-5049*

Texas, Eastern Division	(vcis)	(214) 592-6119
Texas, Western Division	(vcis)	
(includes San Antonio and El Paso)		(210) 229-4023
Utah	(vcis)	(800) 733-6740
	(vcis)	(801) 524-3107
Vermont	(vcis)	(802) 747-7627
Virginia, Eastern District	(vcis)	(800) 326-5879
Virginia, Western District		
Harrisonburg Division		(703) 434-3181
Lynchburg Division		(804) 845-0317
Roanoke Division		(703) 857-2873
Washington, Eastern District	(vcis)	(509) 353-2404
(includes Spokane)		
Washington, Western District	(vcis)	(206) 442-8543
(includes Seattle)		
	(vcis)	(206) 442-6504
West Virginia, Northern District	(vcis)	(304) 233-7318
West Virginia, Southern District	(vcis)	(304) 347-5337
Wisconsin, Eastern District	(vcis)	(414) 297-3582
Wisconsin, Western District	(vcis)	(800) 743-8247
Wyoming		(307) 772-2037

BACKGROUND INVESTIGATIONS

Source Publications publishes what is probably the most comprehensive and useful reference book for any investigator, *The Guide to Background Investigations.*

Expensive (but worth every penny) this 1,000-plus page book lists civil and criminal courts, state and federal agencies, educational institutions, and much more.

(800) 247-8713

BEARAK REPORTS

Provides confidential financial investigations of companies and individuals.

(800) 331-5677; (508) 620-0110

BRB PUBLICATIONS

This company publishes reference books and computer files detailing sources for public records. Their data covers local, state, and Federal courthouses.

(800) 929-3764

BUSINESS BACKGROUND INVESTIGATIONS

Effective way ANY business that has a toll free number can be located by calling. The operators will provide the location.

(800) 555-1212

CDB INFOTEK

This nationwide company can provide public and private records, including credit histories, criminal records, lawsuits, corporations and fictitious business name filings, driving and motor vehicle records, real property records. One stop shopping, by telephone, computer, or fax.

California (800) 427-3747

Outside California (800) 992-7889

CELEBRITY ADDRESSES

Axiom Information Resources provides mailing addresses for celebrities, politicians, athletes, and other famous individuals.

(313) 761-4852

CHILD MOLESTERS

The state of California maintains a (for fee) hotline with information on convicted child molesters. Their operators will tell you (for $10 per call) if a potential babysitter, schoolteacher, whatever, has been registered as a sex offender. A growing number of states have pending legislation of this sort.

(900) 463-0400

COMPUTER SERVICES UNLIMITED, INC.

Provides public records from all 50 states, by computer, fax, or telephone.

(800) 836-2049

CORPORATE RECORDS

This nationwide firm serves as a registered agent for corporations. They offer online computer access to a broad range of corporate records.

(212) 246-5070

CORPORATIONS, STATE DEPARTMENTS OF

Every state has a department of corporations that registers corporations doing business in that state. Their databases contain information on corporate histories, executives, office locations, and more.

CREDIT BUREAUS

There are three major credit bureaus that maintain files on almost every American citizen who has ever engaged in any type of credit transaction.

What information these firms can and will release is governed by the Federal Fair Credit Reporting Act and by various state regulation (some states being tougher than others on privacy rights). Anyone who has credit refused based on a negative report from one of these credit bureaus can obtain a gratis copy of their report; anyone can purchase a copy of their own report, at any time.

Equifax   *(800) 505-1208*

Trans Union (TUC)   *(800) 858-8336*

TRW   *(800) 422-4879*

CRIMINAL RECORDS

The National Crime Information Center (NCIC) maintains a comprehensive nationwide database on criminal histories. However, they only provide this information to authorized law enforcement personnel. Their files cover everything from felony records, wanted persons, missing persons, stolen cars, stolen firearms, stolen license tags, stolen securities, stolen items over a certain dollar value, unidentified persons, and much more.

Although these databases are restricted, anyone convicted of a crime can obtain a copy of their own record from the **Federal Bureau of Investigation**.

(202) 324-5454

Criminal records can often be obtained online from database firms such as:

Datafax   *(512) 928-8192*

Tracer's Worldwide Service   *(800) 233-9766*

CDB Infotek   *(800) 427-3747*

Some states allow access to statewide criminal records without requiring a release from the subject.

Colorado	*(303) 239-4201*
District of Columbia	*(202) 879-1373*
Florida	*(904) 488-6236*
Kentucky	*(502) 227-8713*
Maine	*(207) 624-7000*
Montana	*(406) 444-3625*
Nebraska	*(402) 471-4545*
North Dakota	*(701) 221-5500*
Oklahoma	*(405) 427-5421*
Oregon	*(503) 378-3070*
Pennsylvania	*(608) 266-7314*

CT CORPORATION

Has offices nationwide and acts as the registered agent for service of process for many large corporations.

(800) 237-8552

DATAFAX INFORMATION SERVICES

Provides public and private information including criminal and civil records, driving and motor vehicle records, corporate information and histories, by mail, fax, e-mail, or online.

(512) 928-8192 fax (512) 719-3594

DATAQUICK

Provides real property ownership records for all 50 states, by mail, fax, or computer.

(310) 306-4295; (619) 455-6900

DCS INFORMATION SYSTEMS

Provides date of birth and address information nationwide.

(800) 299-3647

DEATH RECORDS

The Social Security Administration's Master File of Death lists every Social Security death claim in the United States since 1962. This file contains the name of the decedent, Social Security Number, and the Zip Code to which the benefit was sent.

DOCTOR INFORMATION

The American Medical Association Physicians Masterfile database includes addresses, biographies, and disciplinary information on all licensed physicians.

(312) 464-5000

You can determine if a physician has been suspended by the Federal Government for Medicare fraud by telephoning the **Office of the Inspector General**.

(410) 786-5197

The annual publication *Questionable Doctors* lists physicians, dentists, and other health care providers who have been accused of malpractice or other violations by their respective licensing organizations.

(800) 410-8478

DUN & BRADSTREET

America's primary credit reporting company for businesses. They can provide reports with a corporate history, resumés of corporate officers, a description of the company's activities, financial information on revenues and assets, and descriptions of lawsuits, liens, and UCC filings.

(800) 362-3425

EQUIFAX

One of America's three primary credit bureaus with databases containing detailed financial and credit information on millions of citizens.

(800) 456-6432

FEDERAL AVIATION ADMINISTRATION (FAA)

The FAA maintains information on all licensed pilots and other airline personnel.

(405) 954-3205

FEDERAL DISTRICT COURTS

Alabama (Northern)	*(205) 731-1701*
Alabama (Central)	*(205) 223-7308*
Alabama (Southern)	*(205) 690-2371*
Alaska	*(907) 271-5568*
Arizona	*(602) 379-3342*
Arkansas (Eastern)	*(501) 324-5351*
Arkansas (Western)	*(501) 783-6833*
California (Northern)	*(415) 556-3031*
California (Central)	*(916) 551-2615*
California (Southern)	*(213) 894-3533*
Colorado	*(303) 844-3157*
Connecticut	*(203) 773-2140*
Delaware	*(302) 573-6170*
District of Columbia	*(202) 273-0555*
Florida (Northern)	*(904) 942-8826*
Florida (Central)	*(904) 232-2320*
Florida (Southern)	*(305) 536-4131*
Georgia (Northern)	*(404) 331-6886*
Georgia (Central)	*(912) 752-3497*
Georgia (Southern)	*(912) 652-4281*
Hawaii	*(808)-541-1300*
Idaho	*(208)-334-1361*
Illinois (Northern)	*(312)-435-5684*
Illinois (Central)	*(217)-492-4020*
Illinois (Southern)	*(618)-482-9371*
Indiana (Northern)	*(219)-236-8260*
Indiana (Southern)	*(317)-226-6670*
Iowa (Northern)	*(319) 364 2447*
Iowa (Southern)	*(515) 284-6284*
Kansas	*(316) 269-6491*
Kentucky (Eastern)	*(606) 233-2503*
Kentucky (Western)	*(502) 582-5156*

FEDERAL DISTRICT COURTS, continued

Louisiana (Eastern)	*(504) 589-4471*
Louisiana (Central)	*(504) 389-3950*
Louisiana (Western)	*(318) 676-4273*
Maine	*(207) 780-3356*
Maryland	*(301) 962-2600*
Massachusetts	*(617) 223-2600*
Michigan (Eastern)	*(313) 226-7060*
Michigan (Western)	*(616) 456-2381*
Minnesota	*(612) 348-1821*
Mississippi (Northern)	*(601)-234-1971*
Mississippi (Southern)	*(601)-965 4439*
Missouri (Eastern)	*(314)-539 2315*
Missouri (Western)	*(816)-426-2811*
Montana	*(406) 687 6366*
Nebraska	*(402) 221-4761*
Nevada	*(702) 455-4011*
New Hampshire	*(603)-225 1423*
New Jersey	*(201)-645-3730*
New Mexico	*(505)-766 2851*
New York (Northern)	*(518) 472-5651*
New York (Southern)	*(212) 791-0108*
New York (Eastern)	*(718) 330-7671*
New York (Western)	*(716) 846-4211*
North Carolina (Eastern)	*(919) 856-4370*
North Carolina (Central)	*(704) 255-5347*
North Carolina (Western)	*(704) 255-4702*
North Dakota	*(701) 222-6690*
Ohio (Northern)	*(216) 522-4356*
Ohio (Southern)	*(614) 469-5835*
Oklahoma (Northern)	*(918) 581-7796*
Oklahoma (Eastern)	*(918) 687-2471*
Oklahoma (Western)	*(405) 231-4792*
Oregon	*(503) 326-5412*
Pennsylvania (Eastern)	*(215) 597-7704*
Pennsylvania (Central)	*(717) 347-0205*
Pennsylvania (Western)	*(412) 644-3528*
Puerto Rico	*(809) 766-6484*
Rhode Island	*(401) 528-5100*
South Carolina	*(803) 765-5816*
South Dakota	*(605) 330-4447*
Tennessee, Eastern	*(615) 545-4228*
Tennessee, Central	*(615) 736-5498*

FEDERAL DISTRICT COURTS, continued

Tennessee, Western	*(901) 544-3315*
Texas, Northern	*(214) 767-0787*
Texas, Southern	*(713) 250-5500*
Texas, Eastern	*(903) 592-8195*
Texas, Western	*(512) 229-6550*
Utah	*(801) 524-5160*
Vermont	*(802) 951-6301*
Virginia, Eastern	*(703) 557-5131*
Virginia, Western	*(703) 982-4661*
Washington, Eastern	*(509) 353-2150*
Washington, Western	*(206) 553-5598*
West Virginia, Northern	*(304) 636-1445*
West Virginia, Southern	*(304) 342-5154*
Wisconsin, Eastern	*(414) 297-3372*
Wisconsin, Western	*(608) 264-5156*
Wyoming	*(307) 772-2145*
Guam (Territorial Court)	*(671) 472-7411*
Virgin Islands (Territorial Court)	*(809) 774-8310*

FEDERAL BUREAU OF PRISONS

This government agency publishes the *Federal Prison Locator,* which lists everyone who has been incarcerated in a Federal prison since 1981. For information earlier than 1981 check *Federal Prison Archives*, from the same source.

(202) 307-3126

FORTUNE'S BUSINESS REPORTS

Fortune magazine can provide reports that include corporate history, resumés of corporate officers, a description of the company's activities, financial information on revenues and assets, and descriptions of lawsuits, liens, and UCC filings.

(800) 989-4636   *(415) 705-6973*

FREEDOM OF INFORMATION ACT

These two companies can provide assistance in obtaining information from the government under the auspices of the Freedom of Information Act.

Washington Researchers   *(202) 333-3499*

FOIA Clearinghouse   *(202) 785-3704*

INFAQ

A research firm that can provide criminal histories nationwide.
(317) 466-9520

INTELLIGENCE, INC.

(ISECO) offers many books, tools, and equipment for investigations. They also have a "People Trackers" service with an amazing array of available searches. Examples: backgrounds, media references, surname, phone number to address and the reverse, neighbors, PO Box owners, real property by county, consumer credit, bank assets, criminal records, educational background, and a lot more.
(800) 247-6553

INTERNAL REVENUE SERVICE

To verify a business tax identification number.
(209) 456-5900

INVESTIGATOR'S OPEN NETWORK (ION)

This is a nationwide referral service for private investigators.
(800) 338-3463

LAW ENFORCEMENT IDENTIFICATION & INFORMATION MANUAL

Contains full-color photographs of a wide range of IDs (drivers licenses from each state, immigration cards, U.S. passports, military ID cards, and many more).
(714) 498-4815; (800) 498-0911

LEXIS-NEXIS

A nationwide online information provider. Particularly for law firms engaged in both civil and criminal proceedings.
(800) 227-4908; (800) 543-6882; (513) 859-5398

MARINES PERSONNEL LOCATOR

To find a member of the U.S. Marine Corps.
(703) 640-3942

MEDICAL INFORMATION BUREAU

Maintains a database of medical information on anyone who has been hospitalized or medically insured. Restricted to insurance companies but individuals may obtain copies of their own files
(617) 426-3660

METRONET

Provides database searches by telephone, including nationwide surname scans, reverse directory, and Social Security tracking. Note that this is a 900-call, and costs about $2.50 per minute.
(900) 288-3020

MILITARY RECORDS

The personnel files of former military personnel are housed at The National Personnel Records Center.
(314) 263-3901

MILITARY INFORMATION ENTERPRISES, INC.

Can obtain the records of former military personnel, which can be a formidable task for an individual. One executive of this company wrote a highly useful book (at bookstores or check with your library), titled *How To Locate Anyone Who Is or Has Been in the Military.*
(800) 937-2133

MVR SERVICES

Maintains a nationwide database of driving records and vehicle ownership.
(800) 288-6877

NAVY PERSONNEL LOCATOR

To find a service member of the U.S. Navy.
(703) 614-3155

PHONEDISC POWERFINDER

Digital Directory Assistance, Inc. offers practically every telephone book in the country, in CD-ROM format. Titled the ***Phonedisc Powerfinder***, you simply enter an area code and telephone to produce an address, or enter the address and produce the telephone number.
(800) 284-8553

PHYSICIANS MASTERFILE

The American Medical Association physicians masterfile database includes addresses, biographies, and disciplinary information on all licensed physicians.
(312) 464-5000

P.I. MAGAZINE

Billed as "America's Private Investigation Journal," *P.I. Magazine* is a quarterly publication for private investigators. Contains many ads for licensed private investigators, databases, and other information resources. Check out their Internet website at: `http://www.pimall.com`
(419) 382-0967

POLICE REPORTS

Nationwide criminal reports can be obtained from **Regional Report Services**.
(800) 934-9698

SCREEN ACTOR'S GUILD

If you're seeking information on celebrities, the Screen Actor's Guild is the primary information union that represents film and television actors and actresses. The union's office can help you locate members of the guild.

(213) 954-1600

SHOMER-TEC

Sells a comprehensive array of investigative and surveillance equipment, books, and gadgets.
(360) 733-6214

SOCIAL SECURITY NUMBER VERIFICATION

The Social Security Administration will verify the legitimacy of a Social Security Number but only to an employer who has already hired the person who provided the SSN in question. The employer must provide the Administration with the company's Federal Tax Identification Number, as well as the full name, Social Security Number, and date of birth of the employee.
(800) 772-1213

THE SOURCEBOOK OF ONLINE PUBLIC RECORD EXPERTS

Covers proprietary databases, gateway vendors, CD-ROM providers, national and regional search firms, online private investigators, pre-employment and tenant screening specialists, etc. Costs $29.
(800) 929-3810

TRACERS WORLDWIDE SERVICES

Will do searches in *Questionable Doctors* for a fee.
(800) 233-9766

TRANS REGISTRY LIMITED

Maintains a database that identifies and tracks problem tenants, and is a valuable tool for landlords. Offered on a subscription basis, their information can be accessed by telephone or online.
(202) 662-1233

TRANS UNION

One of the three main credit history bureaus.

(800) 858-8336

TRW REDI PROPERTY DATA

Probably the largest database of real estate ownership listings, property maps, and aerial photographs. Most of their database can be accessed by modem.

(800) 421-1052

UNIQUE PUBLICATIONS FOR RESOURCES AND REFERENCE

Lee Lapin's book *The Whole Spy Catalog* is an amazing resource for researchers, PI's, spies, and just plain nosy people. The ultimate guide for finding information and intelligence on almost anything. More than 400 pages on the latest and best hardware, software, techniques, resources, manufacturers, publications, and much more. $49.95 and worth every penny.

(800) 546-6707

A brilliant book concept is *The Investigator's Little Black Book*, by Robert Scott, a well known private investigator. Its cover says "Hundreds and Hundreds and Hundreds of Inside Sources for Investigative Professionals." Organized alphabetically by topic, it covers almost every name and description of services, plus telephone number, for anyone seeking hard to find or confidential information, all for only $19.95.

(800) 546-6707

Index